Jonah the Woodchopper

Encouraging Stories for Finding Your Way Through the Forest of Life

by
Joshua Rubin

D1606553

PENLIGHT PUBLICATIONS
New York

*Jonah the Woodchopper: Encouraging Stories for
Finding Your Way Through the Forest of Life*
by Joshua Rubin

Book design by Ariel Walden

First Edition. Printed in Israel.
ISBN 978-0-9838685-1-4
Library of Congress Control Number: 2012938851

Penlight Publications
527 Empire Blvd.
Brooklyn, NY 11225 U.S.A.
Tel: 718-288-8300
Fax: 718-972-6307
www.PenlightPublications.com

Distributed by Independent Publishers Group

Contents

Encouragement as You Walk
Through the Forest of Life

Better Attitudes Award You a Happier Life

To the Reader

THERE ARE TWO ways to read *Jonah the Wood-chopper*. The first way is to pause after each story and do the story's exercises. You will recognize the exercises as they appear in a different font. The second way is to read through the stories and afterwards go back and do the exercises. Here are a few guidelines for the exercises:

The purpose of the exercises:

The exercises are intended to encourage you on your journey of moving your life forward.

In the exercises you will find:

1. Writing exercises to help you personalize each story's message.

2. Exercises designed to give yourself the encouragement you need in order to improve your life.

3. Affirmations to empower you on your journey forward.

How to use the Messages and/or Affirmations:

The message of each story is summed up at the end of each story.

1. The stories' messages and affirmations are written in a concise form so they may be used during personal reflection or meditation. To do so, find a quiet place to sit, close your eyes, breathe normally and repeat the message and/or affirmation over and over. Even without experiencing an immediate change in the specific issue you are dealing with, repeating the message and/or affirmation will encourage you and make you more aware of the strength you have to improve your life.

The benefit of repeating the message and/or affirmation is based on the theory of autosuggestion, which explains that we possess the strengths needed to improve our lives, yet we need to constantly remind ourselves of these strengths.

2. Write the message/affirmation and tape it to your computer, refrigerator door, work desk, etc. Let this message be a reminder of what you want to focus on.

3. Use the message/affirmation with friends. For example, at a dinner, read the story aloud and then share the story's message/affirmation. Go around the room and have people

share how they understand the message/affirmation or how it is relevant to their lives.

4. Use the story's message/affirmation as an inspiration for a writing exercise. To do so:

Write the sentence on the top of your page.

Keep staring at the sentence and repeating it in your mind until your own words begin to flow through your pen. Try not to censor your writing. Whatever comes up, even if seemingly unrelated to the message/affirmation, is precious, and it is what you need to share with yourself.

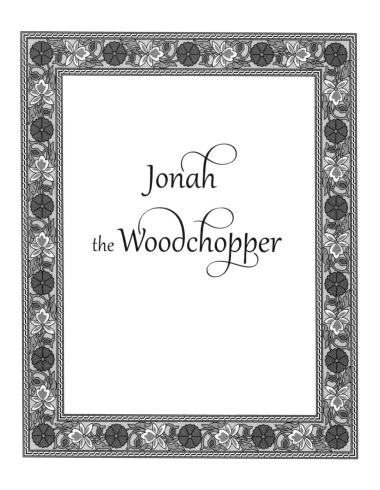

Jonah
the Woodchopper

Jonah's Beginning

(O) UT OF THE woods came a man. Looking at him, it was plain to see that the man had not slept indoors for a very long time. The man approached the Village Elder and asked him, "Can I stay?"

"Can you work?" asked the Village Elder.

"I can chop wood," replied Jonah.

"Then we are happy you are here," the Village Elder said with a welcoming smile and handshake.

Jonah was a quiet person, an extremely quiet person. Jonah chose to live on the edge of the village, right where the forest began. Close to the village, yet close enough to the forest if he felt he needed to hide himself away.

David was a young boy who lived in the village. At age eleven, he was orphaned when his parents succumbed to cholera. David came to see this newcomer. Jonah was chopping wood when he noticed David, but he kept silent. Finally, David said, "Why are you here?"

Jonah wasn't sure he wanted to respond. Yet he saw his own loneliness in David's face. Jonah thought to himself,

I came out of the woods to share, but am I ready to talk to people?

David waited and when Jonah didn't answer, he asked again, "Why are you here?"

This book is Jonah's answer to David's question.

You Can

Find

Encouragement

Finding Sparks

D) AVID WENT TO school every morning. And every afternoon, when school was over, he would run to spend time with Jonah. David was so happy that Jonah had chosen to live so close to the forest. David loved to see the swaying branches and took pleasure in the slight chill he felt when the wind blew through the trees. David said, "I think I know why you like living so close to the forest."

"Why, David?" Jonah asked.

"Because this place is so beautiful!" David exclaimed.

"Yes, David, that is true, but there is also another reason. You see, David, a long time ago, I knew a boy who wanted to become a blacksmith. His parents agreed and arranged for him to be apprenticed to a blacksmith. He diligently learned all the essential techniques of the trade, like how to hold the tongs, how to lift the sledge, how to strike the anvil, and even how to intensify the fire by blowing on it with the bellows. He finished his apprenticeship, and opened his own shop, but had trouble getting his work started. This was because he had not learned how to kindle a spark. You see, David, I live close to the forest because I know this is where my sparks are. The sparks I need to give light to my day."

—————————— *Message* ——————————

We need to find and go to those places and those people that inspire and ignite the sparks within us.

Writing Exercise

- Where do you go to find your sparks?

- Who helps you get your sparks?

- What helps you get your sparks – DVDs, books, music, internet, etc.?

- How would you feel if you were able to reconnect with your sparks?

- Repeat the following affirmation: "I deserve to reconnect to my sparks."

- In what areas of your life would you see improvement if you were to reconnect with your sparks? Try to notice both the small and large improvements.

- When was the last time you allowed yourself to visit your sparking place or spend time with someone or something that gives you inspiration? Write down the date and year. Now make a plan with a time and date to visit your sparking place or person in the very near future.

_____ Affirmations _____

I deserve to reconnect to my sparks.

I know where to go to find my sparks.

I feel full of inspiration.

The Hum

D AVID BEGAN TO help with the chopping. This time, as they chopped, David let his mind wander. After a long while, he slowly began to realize that he was hearing music, as if someone was singing. As David continued to listen, he was surprised to discover that this music, which was actually more like a hum, was coming from Jonah himself.

David asked Jonah, "Why are you humming?"

"David, I didn't even realize I was humming, but it is a good thing and it is proof that I made the right decision to leave the woods and come live near the village." David wanted to ask for an explanation but had learned to wait to see if Jonah was willing to talk.

After a while Jonah remarked, "It is something I learned from my grandfather. A long time ago he taught me a beautiful song, and every time he saw me, my grandfather would sing it to me. When he was about to leave this world, my grandfather called me to his bedside and asked me, 'Jonah, do you remember the song I taught you?'

"'Of course I do, Grandfather. I could never forget your song.'"

"'Listen, Jonah. Throughout your lifetime you are going to make very important decisions and I will not be there to give you advice. But if you make a decision and you can still remember our song, that will be the sign that you have made the right decision!'

"So, David, without even knowing it, I was humming my grandfather's song. This must mean I made the right decision to leave the forest and maybe I am getting ready to share."

———————— *Message* ————————

Music has the power to connect us to our inner selves where we find clarity about which direction we want to lead our lives.

Exercise

EXERCISE ONE:

Ask yourself, what music inspires you and how often do you listen to it?

Choose one inspirational song/piece of music. For one week, listen to the song everyday or, alternatively, read the lyrics.

Keep the lyrics in your pocket and turn them into a prayer or affirmation.

After listening to the song, read the lyrics and write down your thoughts.

EXERCISE TWO:

Pay attention to how often and when you sing during the day.

Notice the positive changes in your life, as you add more singing to your daily routine.

Affirmations

Singing adds happiness and
encouragement to my daily routine.

Singing opens my heart.

Singing connects me to my feelings.

Singing soothes me.

I enjoy singing.

Clearing Ground

THE NEXT DAY, when David came to see Jonah, he did not find him at his cabin, so he went looking for him. At last, he found him. Jonah was standing in a very rocky part of the forest.

"What are you doing here?" David asked.

"I am clearing the ground to plant more trees," Jonah replied.

"But, Jonah, this part of the forest is so rocky, there must be hundreds if not thousands of rocks here! You cannot possibly clear them all!"

"Maybe not," Jonah remarked as he reached down and picked up another stone. "But I can clear this one and this one and this one, too."

David helped Jonah clear some of the stones and when it became late, he walked back to the village. As he was walking away, David thought he heard Jonah repeating to himself, "This one and this one and this one and this one. . ."

———— Message ————

Focus on what you can do.

Exercise

Clearly, no one can deal with all their issues all the time, but all of us can do something, some of the time.

Make a chart with two columns.

In one column, list the big issues you are dealing with in your life, relationships, or work.

In the second column, write one small baby step you can take to work through the issue.

For now, do not focus on solving your larger issues. Just focus on the next small action you can take.

Remember, taking action is more effective than doing nothing. Small baby steps can be a catalyst for change.

———— Affirmations ————

I am focused on what I can do.

Focusing on what I can do motivates
me to move forward.

Awake at Night

THE NIGHTS WERE difficult for Jonah. When the village's commotion quieted down, he felt a restlessness awakening inside of him. The quiet allowed too much room for the unsettling voices from his past. Feeling nervous, Jonah found himself roaming around without going in any particular destination.

Late as it was, Jonah saw that the shoemaker's light was still flickering. Jonah knocked at the door and was welcomed in. Jonah asked, "Samuel, why you are working so late?"

Samuel put down his hammer, cupped his hand around the small stump of candle and answered, "As long as the candle is burning, it is still possible to fix," and he returned to mending a pair of shoes.

Jonah bade Samuel a good night and walked home wondering, *could I fix my past?* Jonah was hoping that as long as his candle burned, he too could fix himself.

———— Message ————

As long as the candle is burning,
it is still possible to fix.

Exercise

As long as we are alive, we have a candle burning inside ourselves. This may sound like wishful thinking until we focus on the fact that our internal body temperature is 98.6°F/37°C. In fact, there are people who do not feel cold in winter because they are so well-connected to their internal heat source.

In spiritual language, this internal heat source is called the soul, which is our source of energy and vibrancy. It is from this energy source, the soul, that we find the strength to fix our lives. When we are feeling down or unsure of our strength, we can reconnect to our internal heat-energy soul-source through sharing love, singing, dancing and meditation.

Practicing any of the above reconnects us to our internal candle.

Once a week, light a candle, stare at it for a few minutes and spend time with the candle. The candle is a physical reflection and represents the candle you have burning inside yourself.

Write a composition titled "My Internal Candle." Start by listing five words that come to mind when you hear the word "candle."

Continue by listing five words that come to mind when you hear the word "internal."

Read your two lists out loud.

Begin your essay by using your "Candle" and "Internal" words.

——————— *Affirmations* ———————

I feel my soul warming me like a candle.

I have the power to fix my life.

Becoming a Miracle

JONAH AND DAVID spent most of their days in silence. They would fall into a rhythmic pattern with their axes rising and falling while chopping wood. Jonah and David would go on like that for a long time without uttering a single word. Usually, David broke the silence.

"Jonah," David began "We spend our days chopping wood. We place the wood on the stump and then, axe up, and axe down, hour after hour. Jonah, I feel nothing special is ever going to happen to me."

"David, sounds like it's time for a break and a story."

They stepped over to their wooden stumps and sat down.

"David, there is a story about a man to whom something very special happened. The first thing you need to know is that this person was very generous – so generous, that whenever he saw the community's charity collectors, he would give them everything he had in his pockets."

"You are joking, right, Jonah?" David interjected.

"No I am not, David. He gave them everything! It got to the point that when the charity collectors saw the man, they felt so bad leaving him penniless that they would run away.

"One day he went to the village to buy a dowry for his

daughter. You know sheets, pillows, blankets, and things like that. Suddenly, he saw the charity collectors. They saw him and ran away, but he ran after them and stopped them. He asked why they were collecting. They answered, 'There is a young woman, an orphan, getting married and we are collecting money for her dowry.' Sure enough, he gave them everything he had just bought for his daughter, saying, 'I can take care of my daughter, but the orphan has got no one to help her.' After giving everything away, he remained with two bits. With the coins, he bought some hay for the horses. When he got home, he put the hay in the barn and told his daughter what had happened.

"A little while later, his wife came home and asked the daughter, 'Where is the dowry?' The daughter, with a heavy sigh, said 'Everything father bought, he put in the barn.' Her mother, not really understanding why her daughter was troubled, went to the barn to discover that the barn was stuffed to the very top with hay. God had performed a miracle and turned the two bits worth of hay into thousands of coins worth of hay.

"You see, David, the man was charitable in a very special way. He never held back, so God responded by not holding back. David, if we want a miracle to happen, we have to become a miracle. If we want something special to happen to us, we have to become something special."

_____ Message _____

If you want something special to happen to
you, you have to do something special.

_____

Exercise

Suggestions for making something special happen in your life:

- Help someone in an extraordinary way.
- Make an extraordinary commitment to do volunteer work.
- Become an expert in something. Start with something small, like napkin folding, or learn all there is to know about some trivia subject, and work your way up.
- Plan a unique weekend for yourself or a loved one.
- Learn about outstanding people. Let their lives inspire you.
- Set yourself a difficult goal and aspire to reach it.

_____ Affirmation _____

I have the power to do extraordinary things.

———————————— ⚜ ————————————

The Power

DAVID ANXIOUSLY WAITED at the carving tree for Jonah's return. David not only missed spending time with Jonah, but he also looked forward to seeing the glow in Jonah's face when he came back from visiting with his elder. David was a little bit jealous of that glow.

"I see you had a good lesson," David said, walking in step with Jonah on their way back to the cabin. Jonah just turned his face towards David and smiled. David continued, "I know why you are so happy."

"Why is that?" Jonah asked.

"Because when you are with your teacher, you feel that he loves you."

"Yes, of course, you are right," Jonah said. "However, there is also another reason. When I am with my teacher, he makes me feel that I have the power to love everyone else."

——————— *Message* ———————

A teacher for life is one who makes you feel
that you have the power to love other people.

Exercise

Seek out a teacher who will support, love, and empower you
to the extent that this person will give you the power to love
others, even people that are difficult to love.

_____ Affirmation _____

I have the power to love.

———————— ⚜ ————————

The Test of Broken Promises

D) AVID WANTED TO know, "Jonah, how did you come to learn with your Elder?"

"Well, living in the forest, I would spend many nights near a fire warming myself. Travelers were often attracted to my fire. They would sit with me and tell me stories. One of the stories was of a special Elder and as soon as I heard the story they told about him, I knew he was the Elder for me."

Not allowing Jonah to slip back into silence David prompted: "And the story?"

"This story starts of with the harshness of life. In a village there was a husband who worked cleaning stables. It was hard and smelly work. After work he would go to the inn to drink and try to forget. Sad as it is, at home he would take out his frustrations on his wife, by sometimes beating her. When the Village Elder heard about this he said to her, 'I will help you get away,' and they made up a plan to meet late at night in the woods by her cabin.

"The Elder came early to make sure not to miss her. 11:00 passed, so did 12:00 and 1:00 in the morning. In fact the Elder waited the whole night but she didn't show. The next day the Elder met her in the marketplace and she assured him, 'Tonight I will come.' Yet once again 11:00 passed, so did 12:00 and she didn't show. The third day they met once again in the marketplace and again she promised 'Tonight I will meet you. Tonight I will leave him. Tonight I will start my life all over again. Just wait for me, I can't do this on my own.'

"Again the Elder came, this time with a blanket just in case she didn't show, and again she didn't come. Her promises were the same on the fourth day and when the Elder brought a blanket and a flask to keep him warm. But this time he didn't need them because the woman appeared at 11:00 and together they walked to a nearby village where she would be safe from her husband's beatings.

"As they walked, the wife said, 'I know I owe you an explanation and even an apology. I saw you on the first night and I was ready to go, but I wasn't sure you were really going to help me. I have had so many people let me down. Again on the second night I saw you waiting. I saw how cold you were, but I wasn't sure you were really going to stand by me and help me. On the third night, I almost came. Really, I almost came, but it was like a voice inside frightened me. Maybe I was too frightened to hope. But when you came back on the fourth night, even after I had let you down and broke my promises, then it was clear to me that you would never leave until I came, and then I knew I could trust you to help me.'

"You see, David, I needed an Elder who understood that many times we break promises not because we are bad people, but because we are testing. Testing if you will still love me, if you will still stand by me when I let you down. I needed such a person to get me out of the forest and to begin to trust people once again."

———————— *Message* ————————

Some people test how much we love and
trust them by breaking their promises.

Exercise

Parents know the secret of trusting people who break their promises through their experience with their own children. Children apologize, promise not to do it again; parents give them a second chance hoping their children will own up to their promises, yet knowing that there is a good chance they won't. When the child once again breaks the trust given by his parents, once again the child apologizes and once again the parents give the child another chance. This is a long, ongoing process ending when the child is finally ready to be responsible and trustworthy to keep their promises. Part of the reason that our children keep breaking their promises is they are testing whether we will still love them if they act this way.

There are times when emotional duress causes us or others to act just like our children. We break people's trust in us knowing we are risking the relationship, yet hoping that we will still be loved even though we have disappointed the other.

This story asks us:

- How many times can we forgive?
- How many times can we reopen our hearts after hurt has sealed them?
- How many times can we trust someone after they have disappointed us?

Remember that it is easy to forgive someone who hasn't hurt your feelings and to trust someone who hasn't broken your trust. Here the exercise is to help us again trust someone that has disappointed us.

This exercise begins with a word association. Write the word "trust" on the top of your page. Then free associate and write the first five words that you connect with the word trust. Write a sentence for each word. Repeat the word association, this time using the word "promise."

Afterwards think about, discuss, or write down your answers to these questions:

- Who taught you about trust?
- What three promises have you kept?
- What three promises have you broken?
- Were you forgiven for breaking someone's trust? If so, why did they forgive you? Is there someone who has broken their promise to you?

- Why is it so difficult to forgive them?
- What would need to happen internally and externally for me to trust this person once again?

_____ *Affirmations* _____

I can trust again.

I open my heart.

———————— ⚜ ————————

(This advice should be disregarded in the case of an abusive relationship, and does not preclude one from seeking professional, physiological, or physical care.)

The Hug

JONAH AND DAVID were strolling through the Village. In front of the village tavern sat Joseph, the village drunk. People called Joseph "The Drunkard" because when he was not earning a few coins for a drink, he was drinking. Joseph's eyes lit up when he saw Jonah. "Did you bring my present?" Joseph asked.

"I did," replied Jonah. "But you know, Joseph, you have to stand up to receive it." David didn't recognize this Joseph, who was standing up so straight and looking so proud. Jonah stepped closer to Joseph, put his arms around him, and hugged him.

To which Joseph said, "Thank you, Jonah," and sat down, holding his drink.

As they walked away, David asked, "Jonah, why is it that every day you go up to Joseph and hug him?"

Jonah leaned against a tree as if to draw courage from its strength. "David," he began, "there was a time when I did not live here, in this village. In fact, I did not live anywhere except in the forest itself. I hunted, bathed in the streams, and when I could find it, I drank until I forgot that I did not have any place to call my own. One day, an Elder approached me and asked me, 'Are you ready to receive your present?' I said, 'Sure!'

"The man said, 'But you know you have to stand up to

36

receive your present.' Having nothing to lose, I stood up and he hugged me, whispering in my ear, 'You can save someone's life with just one hug,' and he walked away.

"It was soon after this event that I, at last, found the courage to come down into this village and begin to make a living, chopping wood. You see, David, his hug saved me," and Jonah looked over his shoulder at Joseph and prayed, "Maybe, just maybe. . ."

────────── *Message* ──────────

You can save someone's life with just one hug.

─────────────────────────

Exercise

Each day make sure you hug your partner and children.
When greeting your friends, with their permission, start hugging them.
If you see someone in need, and your inner voice tells you a hug would really cheer him or her up, trust your inner voice.

────────── *Affirmations* ──────────

I love hugging people.

I have the power to lower barriers
between myself and other people.

────────── ⚜ ──────────

Getting Out of Holes

JOSEPH, THE VILLAGE drunk, raised his glass and said, "You know, Jonah, you should not spend so much time with me here in the tavern. With your drinking history, it is dangerous for you to be here!"

Jonah looked down at his glass of water and said, "Thank you, Joseph, for your concern, but you are here and I want to spend time with you. Besides, I find the strength to be here because of a story my father once told me."

Jonah went on, "A man was walking down the street, and he was not very careful about where he was going. All of a sudden, he felt himself falling into a deep pit with walls so high, he could not climb out. A doctor walked by and the man yelled out for help, but the doctor just wrote him a prescription, threw it into the pit, and kept on walking. Then, a religious individual walked by. The man yelled, 'I fell into this hole. Can you help me get out?' The religious person wrote a prayer, threw it into the pit, and kept on walking. Some time later, his good friend, Reuben, happened to walk by the pit. The man yelled out, 'Reuben, I fell into this hole. Can you help me?' Reuben heard his friend's plea for help and jumped into the hole! 'Reuben, are you crazy? Now, we are both down in this pit!' 'True,' said Reuben, 'But I have been down here before and I know the way out!'"

——————————— *Message* ———————————

People who have been through my difficulty can
help me get through what I am dealing with.

———————————————————————————

Exercise

When dealing with any difficulty, seek out people who have been in your dilemma and have successfully dealt with the problem. Even if their coping mechanisms may not work exactly for you, you can still learn a lot from their struggles and successes.

——————— *Affirmation* ———————

I reach out to friends who comfort me.

————————— ⚜ —————————

The Warmest Fire

JONAH AND JOSEPH were in the forest. They were sitting close to the fire, warming their bodies and their souls.

Joseph looked at his flask and reflected, "Jonah, just tell me that one day it will be all right. I know you stopped your drinking. Jonah, just tell me that it will be all right and that one day, I, too, will stop drinking."

Jonah retorted, "Joseph, how can I tell you that it will be all right? Am I a prophet who knows the future?"

In disgust, Joseph said, "then what good are you!"

Jonah reached over, held out his hand and said to Joseph, "I cannot make you any promises, but I can be with you in your darkness."

———————— *Message* ————————

Holding someone's hand in their time of
difficulty is very strong medicine.

———————————————————

Exercise

We know the power of kind and supportive words when we want to help someone in their difficulty. Yet sometimes we overlook the importance of silently holding a person's hand. This is also true when we seek help. Sometimes we need advice, but many times all we need is someone to hold us without talking. When all we need is holding, it is crucial that we share this with our friend or partner: "Right now, I do not want or need advice. All I need and want is to be held."

———— Affirmation ————

I have the fortitude to be with
someone in his or her pain.

⚜

The Four Candles

JOSEPH WANTED TO know, "Jonah, where do you get the strength to spend time with me when everyone else has given up hope that I will ever change?"

"Joseph, I had the good fortune to hear my father tell me a story which has stayed with me my entire life.

"A father gave his son a beautiful toy house. The house was rectangular with walls of glass. Its roof had two round brass chimneys which allowed the four candles inside to burn brightly.

"The father said, 'These are special candles. We have to make sure they don't go out.'

"The boy placed the candles on the dresser facing his bed so he could watch them as he fell asleep, and could wake up first thing to their brilliance.

"At the same time, while watching the candles, the boy could sometimes hear his parents fighting. This went on for a few days.

"One night as he stared at the candles, the first candle whispered to him, 'My name is Peace. Too many people can't keep me lit so maybe I should go away,' and the candle went out. The boy was very sad.

"The next night, as he spent time with his candles, he

heard his father tell his mother, 'Things are never going to get better.'

"Then the second candle whispered to him, 'My name is Belief, but not too many people believe in me anymore. Maybe it is better if I just go away,' and the candle went out. The boy was very sorry to lose that candle.

"The next night the boy felt a little cold with only two candles burning, but was happy that they still gave off their light. Warming his fingers with the warmth that was left, he heard his mother ask his father 'Where did our love go?'

"The third candle very quietly whispered, 'My name is Love, but people stop looking for me so maybe it is best if I go away,' and the candle went out. The boy lay down on his bed and cried.

"The next night the boy was too scared to spend time with the last candle. He thought, *What if the last candle goes out?* The boy listened to his parents speaking in the other room. They said, 'We can try again,' 'We got lost, but we still love each other,' and 'As long as we are together there is hope.'

"The last candle said in a strong proud voice, 'My name is Hope and I have the power to relight the other candles.' The boy lifted up Hope, lit the other three candles, and the light from the glass house filled his room and his heart.

"Hope, Joseph. I have no proof, but I know that holding on to Hope gives hope."

_____ *Message* _____

Hope has the power to relight our lives.

_____

Exercise

When life gets tough, reconnect to:

- People who love you
- People who see the good in you
- People who value your uniqueness
- Positive people

You can also light a candle and place a card in front of it with the word Hope written on it.

_____ *Affirmations* _____

I know where to find hope.

I am hopeful.

Hope makes all things possible.

——————— ⚜ ———————

Advice

THE VILLAGE ELDER came to see Jonah. "Jonah, I understand that you have been helping David and Joseph."

"All we do is chop wood," said Jonah.

"But," the Village Elder continued, "they told me about your advice."

"Advice is like rain," Jonah remarked. "If the rain falls on the earth, it helps the grass to grow, but if the rain falls on rocks, it has little effect."

The Village Elder understood Jonah's parable, and after this, he began sending people to Jonah for his counsel.

—————— Message ——————

*Advice is like rain. If the rain falls on earth,
it helps the grass grow. However, if the
rain falls on rock, it has little effect.*

Exercise

There is much advice floating around in the world. What advice do you need?

STAGE ONE:

Most people know what advice they need, yet many do not trust their own inner voice. In this exercise, imagine that you are sitting with a good friend, mentor, or sage, and you are asking them for their advice to help improve your life. Make sure you write down the advice they would give you. Alternatively, you can imagine the advice you would give to a friend if they had your same issues. Writing down the advice will make it more concrete and tangible. By imagining advice received from a friend or sage, or giving advice to a friend, you are tapping into your own inner voice, for we usually know what we need, yet are wary of trusting our own emotional growth and healing.

STAGE TWO:

"Advice is like rain. If the rain falls on the earth, it helps the grass grow."

Often, the issue is not what advice I need, but that I remain hard like a rock upon which rain, i.e., advice, has little effect, instead of being like earth, ready to absorb the rain of advice.

There are significant events in life that open us up to advice, such as births, deaths, marriages, divorces, dismissal, financial gains, and/or financial needs. One of the important secrets of life is being open to advice, without the necessity of a turbulent life-event.

In this case, the exercise is one of intention. I announce

to myself that I am open to advice. You may decide to post your intention on your refrigerator or your computer, or wherever is good for you – to serve as a constant reminder.

 Affirmations

I am open to advice.

When I am open to advice, I will
be sent the advice I need.

I am like earth, open to receive the
rain that will help me grow.

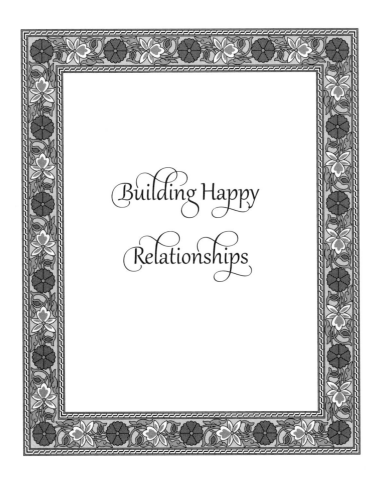

Building Happy

Relationships

The First Lesson

JEREMIAH WAS THE new schoolteacher in the village. He had heard about Jonah and went to consult with him. "Jonah, tomorrow is my first day teaching school and I have seen how all the children love spending time with you and listening to your stories. Do you have any advice for me?"

Jonah said, "Let me tell you about my first day in school, so many years ago. I was small for my age and more than a bit scared when my mother left me at school. I saw the teacher sitting behind his desk. When he saw me, he stood and I thought he was a giant. His black hat, long black coat, and black beard made him look even scarier. He showed me where to sit and I waited for school to begin. After everyone arrived, the teacher said in a loud voice, 'Everyone, in his turn, will go to the back room.' He pointed to the room. 'You will knock politely and enter. Each one of you will then have your first lesson.'"

Jonah continued, "My last name begins with an *a* - Applebaum - so he called my name first. I went to the door, knocked, and he told me to come in. He was standing and he looked very big to me. He told me to come close. I did as I was told. He asked me, 'Are you ready for your first lesson?'

"To tell you the truth," Jonah said to Jeremiah, "I wasn't so sure, but anyway, I said yes.

"The teacher then took a step closer, placed his hands on my head, closed his eyes and said, 'May God protect you. May God bless you and educate you. May God's face turn to you and give you peace.'"

Jonah sighed, remembering, and he told Jeremiah, "I knew that blessing because my father would lay his hands on my head every Friday night and say the very same blessing. The teacher hugged me and said, 'Your first lesson is over.'"

─────── *Message* ───────

Make your first impression one of love.

Exercise

At any given moment, we can open or close our hearts. Those who open their hearts experience and share love, and find opportunities to get close, and possibly hug people. However, opening your heart also means opening yourself, in our harsh world, to the probability of experiencing hurt, disappointment, and even pain. You need to make the decision whether you are willing and, just how often you are willing, to pay the price.

My advice is to hug as many people as you can. You will live a happier life.

_____ *Affirmation* _____

I will seize the next opportunity to hug someone.

Burning Notebooks

J "ONAH, THE VILLAGE ELDER sent me to speak with you," said Eli, the owner of the general store. "I told him I am so angry! Do you know why? A hundred reasons," Eli exclaimed. "My horse died, and how am I supposed to make my deliveries? And Simon the banker is now getting his monthly order from the city! And my wife is sick, very sick! And the terrible fire that burnt Joseph's cabin. And my best friend, it is so unfair, Aaron, my best friend is gone and all he had was a pauper's funeral. Hate! That is what I feel. I hate God! I hate Him for all the evil things He lets happen. I told the Elder, but he sent me to you. He said, 'Go to Jonah. He knows about the notebooks.' Notebooks? I asked. But all the Elder would say is notebooks. What notebooks?"

"Eli, you came at the right time. I will show you my notebooks." Eli followed Jonah into his cabin where a fire had been kindled in the fireplace.

Standing near the fire, Jonah took out a notebook and said, "Eli, I too have many complaints, so at the end of each month, I write down all the bad things that God does to me and to our community. I even wrote down all the bad things that happened to you!" Then Jonah placed the notebook in the fire.

Then Jonah took out another notebook and said, "In this notebook, I wrote down all the bad things that I did this past month." Jonah slowly raised his eyes to Heaven and said, "God, I forgave You. Now God, You forgive me." And Jonah placed the second notebook on top of the first.

With misty eyes, Jonah turned to Eli and explained, "We are taught to forgive, but we still carry around notebooks in our hearts, and these notebooks, one day, turn into hate. We not only need to learn to forgive, we also need to learn how to burn our notebooks!"

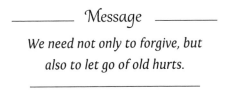

_____ *Message* _____

*We need not only to forgive, but
also to let go of old hurts.*

Exercise

When another person has wronged us, we long for that person's apology. Yet, how can we receive their request for forgiveness when the person who hurt us is not going to ask for our forgiveness, or maybe that person is no longer alive? In such a case, the forgiveness we seek will be a by-product of our healing the hurt that the other has created. When I have healed from the wound that someone else created inside of me, I find the emotional space inside of me to forgive. The shift in thinking is instead of focusing on why the other person should apologize, you are focusing on your own healing process. This is the type of thinking that helps us to burn our notebooks, i.e., to let go of old hurts. The following exercise is helpful in healing emotional wounds and letting go of old hurts. The exercise requires you to write two letters, but do not send either of them. The goal of the letter writing is not to send the letters, but to clear your heart of the negative energy created by being hurt and by carrying around that hurt.

LETTER ONE:
Write a spiteful letter to a person who harmed you. Be petty when you write the letter. Do not be understanding. You may use foul language. Blame the person. Let all your hate, hurt, and pain flow onto the paper. Write how much that person hurt you and the negative affects his/her actions have had on your life.

LETTER TWO:
Write an understanding letter to that same person. Reach up to your higher self and try to understand how much pain that person must have been in to harm you as he /she has done. Write about how much you have healed, how you are no longer the same person that was so devastated. Offer your love and compassion towards the other.

Affirmations

I like to forgive.

I have the power to let go of emotional hurt.

Service of the Heart

ASHER WAS THE postal clerk in the village. One day, Asher went to Jonah and declared in exasperation, "Jonah you have to help me! Feivish is driving me crazy! Every day, he comes to the post office and every day, it is the same routine! Every day, Feivish asks me the same questions over and over, 'Asher, did the mail come in already? When do you expect the mail? You know I am waiting for mail. Asher, are you are sure there is nothing in the mail for me?' Oy, Feivish, Feivish, Feivish!" Asher continued, "Jonah, this happens each and every day! I have no more patience, no more!"

"I understand, Asher, but if heaven made him, earth can find some use for him."

"True, true of course true, but Jonah, in the four months that I have been managing the post office, not one piece of mail has come for him. Feivish is driving me crazy!"

Jonah sighed as he replied, "Yes, I know Feivish and I also know how difficult it is to be as alone as he is. When Feivish visits me, making the same conversation time and time again, I always remember a story my mother told me about my own grandparents.

"She told me about one of the ways my grandparents celebrated the Sabbath. They would invite many, many guests to lunch: sometimes ten, sometimes even twenty. There were always many willing hands to help serve the food, but my grandmother always insisted that she alone serve the stew. While handing each bowl of beans with potatoes, she used this chance to ask each guest who they were and where they came from."

Jonah went on, "One Sabbath, there was a guest at the table who was a little off. You know, he was a little awkward in company. When my grandmother gave him his bowl, he took it, examined it, and said in a very loud voice, 'Potatoes! I cannot stand potatoes! Why did you give me potatoes?' He then took the bowl, flung it in the air, and the whole bowl of stew landed on my grandmother!

"Can you imagine that? The stew, the beans, and everything else in it, was dripping all over my grandmother. Even though this guest was a little disturbed, he realized that he had done something very wrong. He stood up and ran away! My grandmother ran after him! She quieted him down and brought him back to the table, saying, 'It is all right. If you do not want potatoes, I will only give you beans.'

"Later on, after all the guests had left, my mother asked my grandmother, 'Where do you get so much patience for people like that?' Now, Asher, listen carefully to what my grandmother answered – it is what I always think of during Feivish's visits to me. It has helped me very much and it may just help you, too! My grandmother's reply to my mother was, 'When you have compassion in your heart, you do not need patience.'"

─────────── *Message* ───────────

If you have compassion in your heart,
you do not need patience.

───────────────

Exercise

Compassion is created when we realize that two separate people are truly one person, sharing one common humanity. Our common humanity is expressed by the fact that we all tremble before death, and all our hearts soften when we hold newborns. We are all scared of something, and we all have emotional outbursts when we are upset, and it is only the frequency and intensity of those outbursts that differentiate us.

Look at or think about the person toward whom you want to direct your compassion.

Realize that:

Just as you have suffered humiliation as a child, so have they.
Just as you have been yelled at, so have they.
Just as you have been disappointed, so have they.
Just as you have been rejected, so have they.
Just as you have been lonely, so have they.

Just as some of your needs were not met, neither were theirs.
Just as you crave love and acceptance, so do they.
Just as you need to be respected, so do they.

Realize that on the levels of avoiding hurt and of craving love, you are the same.

Allow the compassion you feel for yourself to help you feel compassion for others, and allow the compassion you feel for others to help you feel compassion for yourself.

——————— *Affirmations* ———————

I am a compassionate person.

I have the power to be compassionate.

Sharpening the Axe

JONAH ENJOYED SHARPENING his axe. His attention was captivated by running the steel blade back and forth against the leather strap. There was a centering quality to moving the blade up and down the strap. Jonah was contemplating his thoughts when, suddenly, he was interrupted by Feivish!

"Jonah," he shouted while running from a distance, calling Jonah's name every ten paces. "Jonah," he repeated again, breathing heavily from his quick pace. Feivish reached Jonah and burst out, "Jonah, everyone in the village is so annoying! Everywhere I go, no one has time for me and people are not nice to me. This village is full of rude people! It really disgusts me! Jonah, I want you to give the village people a talking-to!"

Jonah let go of his thoughts and welcomed Feivish."Feivish, good of you to come. I was just sharpening my axe. Would you like to help me?"

Feivish walked over to the sharpening strap hanging from a tree.

"Feivish, hold the free end taut," instructed Jonah. Feivish did and Jonah ran the blade up and down the leather strap.

"Jonah," Feivish began again, but Jonah redirected Feivish's energy, by saying, "Pay attention, Feivish."

After a few more strokes of the blade, Jonah said to him, "Feivish, I understand why you are upset, yet I think you are blaming the wood for being too hard when, really, it is the axe that needs sharpening."

—————— *Message* ——————

Are we blaming our circumstances
for being too hard, when it is actually
ourselves that needs sharpening?

Exercise

List one difficulty you are experiencing in either your personal or professional life. Focus on what you can do to improve your situation, instead of assigning responsibility or blaming another person for your difficulty. Even though such assignment of responsibility may be valid, when we take steps to improve ourselves, others usually follow our lead.

—————— *Affirmation* ——————

I sharpen myself instead of blaming others.

What Is Really Broken?

"JONAH, I THINK I get it. Instead of the axe complaining that the wood is too hard, the axe should make sure it is sharp enough to chop the wood. So instead of me complaining about everyone else, I need to learn to sharpen myself, right?"

Jonah, not wanting to be too harsh with Feivish, asked, "Wouldn't you feel better if your axe was sharp?"

"Maybe you can let me start by sharpening this axe?" So Feivish thought over Jonah's words as he ran the blade up and down the strap.

Finally, he said, "Jonah, can you help me understand the lesson a little better?"

"Feivish, maybe this story will help. A man went to the doctor complaining that his body hurt all over. The doctor asked the man to show him where he hurt. The man pointed to his arm, head, chest, stomach and both his legs. The doctor decided to give the man a thorough examination. After an hour and a half the doctor said, 'I have come to the conclusion that there is nothing wrong with you.' The man asked, 'So why do I hurt all over?' The doctor explained, 'Everything you touched hurts you because your finger is broken.'"

_____ *Message* _____

When a relationship sours ask
yourself, "What was my role?"

Exercise

When a relationship sours, the fault and the fixing never lay with only one side. Fixing begins when each side reflects on how they were both touching the relationship with "broken fingers," i.e., their own conscious and subconscious issues. The more we fix our own issues our "broken fingers" the more clarity we will receive on what went wrong and how we can fix the relationship.

Reflect on a current difficult relationship. Set aside how the other side is contributing to the souring of the relationship. Focus on your contribution to the souring. Ask yourself what would be the first smallest baby step you could take to attempt to rectify the relationship. Take that step!

_____ *Affirmation* _____

I take responsibility for my relationships.

Clean Garbage

D)AVID FOUND JONAH washing his hands in the basin behind his cabin. David suddenly realized that not only were Jonah's hands dirty, but so were his arms, his face, and his head. Even Jonah's clothes were dirty. In fact, Jonah was muddy all over, but that was not the worst of it. Jonah smelled like rotten eggs! "Jonah, what happened to you? You are a mess!" David exclaimed.

"David, I found Joseph, the drunk, in the garbage pit outside the village. He had a little too much to drink, did not watch where he was going, fell in the pit and could not get himself out."

"Jonah, you look like you got down into the pit with him!" David retorted.

"Yes, David, I surely did!" Jonah answered.

"But you know, Jonah, you could have bent down and held out your hand or a branch of a tree, to help pull him up," David countered.

"Of course, you are right, David, but sometimes you need to get into the garbage in order to help the person get out. And, just between you and me, nothing feels cleaner than helping someone out of the garbage!"

——————— *Message* ———————

*Nothing feels cleaner than helping
someone out of the mud.*

———————————————

Exercise

Get dirty helping someone and notice how clean you feel.
   For example:
Look around your immediate surroundings and help a family
   member clean their room, the bathroom, or wash the
   dishes.
Volunteer at a soup kitchen.
Make food for a shelter.
Prune or weed a school's garden.

——————— *Affirmation* ———————

I enjoy helping people.

Where Is the Love?

JONAH WAS SURPRISED to smell her perfume. It was a unique smell and only one family in the village had enough money to buy anything imported and lavish. Jonah prepared for her arrival by placing a towel on top of one of the wooden stumps he used as chairs. Helen understood the gesture, smiled, and sat down.

"Jonah," she began, "Debra, our maid, shared with me what you told her about love. I want to make sure I understood her. She said that you said that:

"'You know you are in love when that certain love, simultaneously, fixes and breaks your heart. That your loved one can bring you up to the highest joy and down to the lowest sadness.

"Yes, that is what I shared with Debra."

"Jonah, tell me, where is this love?" Helen asked, "I know many people who want to be close to me because of my money, but where Jonah, where is this love?"

Jonah sat down on a wooden stump and began to ask her, "Do you remember the Hendels?" Helen nodded yes. "Do you remember when, towards the end, Mrs. Hendel was so sick that she could no longer feed herself?"

Helen said, "Yes, I heard about that."

"Well, when I went to visit them. Mr. Hendel had just

68

gotten back from the general store and had a bag with him. He opened the bag and took out four oranges. Mr. Hendel placed the oranges on the cutting board, sliced them in halves, and squeezed the juice from the oranges into a glass. He then took the glass of orange juice over to where his wife lay, dipped a teaspoon into the glass and, teaspoon by teaspoon, fed his wife her favorite drink. Mr. Hendel then turned to me with tears in his eyes and said, 'Jonah, I thank God that He has allowed me to squeeze fifty years of our relationship into one teaspoon of orange juice.'

"There, Helen, there, in that one teaspoon of orange juice, is the love."

—————————— *Message* ——————————

Love exists and is sustained by small acts of devotion, not necessarily in bombastic overtures.

Exercises

- Give your partner small presents.
- Do small favors for them or small acts of kindness.
- Focus on and address your partner's needs.
- Compliment something specific about your partner and justify your compliment with an example.
- Thank your partner for the small, overlooked actions. For example: Thank you for: doing the laundry, setting the

table, cleaning the car, shopping for groceries, or thank you for getting my favorite soda. Remember, in the end, the love you get is equal to the love you give.

_____ Affirmation _____

I see love in small acts.

I have the power to love through giving.

⎯⎯⎯⎯⎯⎯⎯ ⚜ ⎯⎯⎯⎯⎯⎯⎯

Becoming Your List

AFTER THE HARVEST, when his land lay fallow, Saul would help Jonah prepare the winter stock of wood. Jonah liked working with Saul because Saul understood working in silence. For long stretches, they would fall into a routine of chopping, piling, sharpening the axes and then start all over again. Yet this time, Jonah felt something was bothering Saul. Jonah waited, knowing when Saul was ready he would say his piece. Finally, Saul said, "Jonah, my wife is a very difficult person. How can I get her to change?"

Jonah said, "Saul, you are asking the wrong person."

"Why is that?" Saul asked.

"Because, Saul, my marriage failed," Jonah replied.

"Oh!" was all Saul could think of saying. They fell back into their silent routine until Saul asked, "Can you tell me about your marriage, Jonah?"

"Yes, Saul, I will tell you. Maybe my experience will help your marriage. I was young, haughty, and everything had to be my way. I liked and, even, loved my wife, but she could never fulfill my expectations. I wanted her to be romantic, funny, caring, a good cook, and more. In fact, I even made a list of how I wanted her to change. In the end, she did not meet my expectations and we slowly drifted apart."

"Today," Jonah went on, "I understand where I made my mistake. For a long time, I thought my mistake was making a list, but really, making the list was the first step in the right direction. What I did not understand was what I should have done. I should have written down how I wanted my wife to change and then I should have become my list, and made those changes in myself."

Jonah turned to Saul and he said, "Saul, go and sit down, by yourself, and take some time to think. Write down how you want your wife to change and then you become your list, you make the changes in yourself. I have learned that when we want change to happen in someone else, it is best we start with changing ourselves."

——————— *Message* ———————

*When we want change, we need
to become that change.*

————————————————

Exercise

Make a list of how you want your partner to change and then make those changes in your own behavior or attitude.

Affirmations

I am becoming the change I want in my life.

I am the change I want in my life.

Knotted Love

LISTENING TO JONAH talk about his failed marriage made Saul feel sorry that Jonah came to be so wise only later in life. He asked, "What about today? Would you want to remarry?"

Jonah looked away because he didn't want Saul to see his misty eyes. Saul filled the silence with reassurance, "I am sure there would be many nice women who would love to spend their lives with you."

Jonah felt a lump forming in his throat. Finally he said, "I would like to marry again, but this time I would use the secret of building a log cabin." Jonah pointed to his cabin and asked Saul to take a close look. Saul noticed that most of the planks were not smooth but knotted with grooves.

Saul asked, "Where did you find pieces to exactly match the knots and grooves?"

"I didn't. After placing a knotted plank I would carve grooves and holes in the next plank so it matched the first plank. That way the two planks fit tightly together. When I was younger I tried to straighten out my wife, but today I would accept a woman with her knots and grooves and then I would carve room in myself so we would match perfectly."

———————— *Message* ————————

Love is when you make room in yourself
for other people's needs or interests.

———————————————————

Exercise

Love is the union of two people in thought and feeling. This union of love has two stages: The first stage is finding how much you have in common, how much you enjoy spending time doing things together. People commit to long term relationships if they have achieved this first stage.

During a long-term relationship, one can then experience the second stage of this union of love. The second stage is achieved when you recognize that your partner is different from you, that your partner has different needs and/or interests than you. Then you can expand your love for your partner by supporting and encouraging the pursuit of these differences. It becomes an act of love when you are sensitive to your partner's different needs and make room in your life for your partner's needs.

As a relationship develops, the partners discover a healthy tension of nurturing their common interests while nurturing each other's different interests. This healthy tension can actually be the cause of conflict as you think you are being so loving by offering a foot massage, while your partner wants love expressed by an offer to wash the dishes. This tension can be resolved by practicing "Knotted Love." Here are a few examples of "Knotted Love."

Your expression of love	Your partner's different needs and / or interests
You want to throw your partner a huge surprise birthday party	Your partner wants a small get-together with friends
You find candles romantic	Your partner finds clean sheets romantic
You would like to spend time together by giving a massage	Your partner would rather you use the time to wash the dishes
Discovering a mutual hobby	Your partner can enjoy his or her book club while you go fly fishing

Make a point of discovering what types of expressions of love your partner needs by telling him or her how you would like to express your love, and asking if that is what they would like. Convey that you are open to sharing your love in ways that are meaningful to them.

Affirmations

I am open to my partner's needs.

I am sensitive to my partner's needs.

Lovely Lettuce

DAVID WAS HAPPY to eat supper with Jonah. Supper with Jonah was so much better than eating with the Village Elder, as the Elder was always reading to David from some book. But preparing the food with Jonah was sometimes very annoying. "Jonah, you take too long washing the vegetables. It is as if each vegetable was a gem or something."

"David, sometimes I wash vegetables just as quickly as anyone else, but sometimes I remember how Grandma Rachel would wash her lettuce. I would come by to deliver her wood and she would invite me for lunch. As I sat at her kitchen table, I would watch her separate the leaves of the lettuce and slowly wash each piece. It would take her forever to wash the lettuce. I wouldn't say anything but she sensed my edginess. She turned to me as if she was reading my impatient thoughts and said 'But Jonah I wash each piece of lettuce with love.'

"You see, David, there is a saying 'It is not how much we do, but how much love we put in the doing. It is not how much we give, but how much love we put in the giving.'

"Sometimes I think of Grandma Rachel as I wash the vegetables."

_____ Message _____

Add love to your household tasks.

Exercise

Focus on love or loving while you are washing dishes, doing laundry, and cooking.

You may want to put on relaxing music while you do your household chores and then focus on loving yourself or others. You may get less done, but everything will look and taste better.

_____ Affirmations _____

I am full of love.

I love doing things for other people.

I walk with love.

White Fire

D AVID LIKED THE stillness he felt in Jonah's cabin. He noticed how simple Jonah's home was. A table, two wooden chairs, a bed, a sink, a curtainless window, and a fireplace with a pot of stew simmering over it. What always caught David's interest was Jonah's prized possession – a letter from Jonah's father. Jonah had placed it on the mantelpiece, right above the fireplace. Jonah's father had given this letter to him when he left home.

When David asked him about it, Jonah explained, "When I left home, my father gave me a letter and told me, 'All my love that I have for you, I have put into this letter.' David, when I wake up and before I go to sleep, I look at my father's letter, knowing that with all the friction between us, my father never stopped loving me."

David said, "I wish my parents could have left me such a letter, but they died so quickly when they got sick." Jonah took both of David's hands into his own, placed them on his heart, and said to David, "Now, we have each other, David."

David ate many meals in Jonah's cabin. As he ate, his gaze wandered. Yet his interest always returned to the letter on the mantelpiece. *I wish I had a letter like that,* David thought to himself. He wondered, *How does one put all their love into one letter?* There were even times when Jonah would step over to the mantelpiece, open the letter and smile, but David could never see what was written in the letter, even though, at times, he tried to peek.

Boys will be boys and curiosity can be overwhelming, which is why David made sure Jonah was in the village buying cornmeal and flour when he decided to go to Jonah's cabin. David's heart was pounding when he knocked because although he knew Jonah was not at home he also knew that he was about to break Jonah's trust in him. "Jonah," David called out as he opened the door, knowing there would be no answer, yet anxious that there might be one. Quietly, David approached the mantelpiece, touched the letter, held it gently in his fingers, went back to the door to make sure no one was around and then, very carefully, opened the letter.

"All my love, all my love, all my love, that I have for you, I have put in this letter." Those were the words that David kept repeating in his mind, "All my love, all my love." David was surprised, for the letter was blank, bare of anything written. It was just a clean sheet of white paper. David held the empty sheet up to the sun, hoping. . . but there was nothing written, nothing at all. Suddenly, David understood. It was too heartbreaking for Jonah to tell David the truth, so he made up the story and what a great story it was – a son, a father, and all his love. David concluded that to be able to hold your father's entire love in one letter was really too good to be true.

David went along with the charade the next time he saw Jonah smile as he looked at the letter. He kept Jonah's secret for a while, but once, when he was feeling very lonely, he no longer had the strength to lie about that kind of love, the very kind he wanted to hold in his own hands. David blurted out, "Enough, Jonah, I know there is nothing in the letter! I know you will be mad at me for breaking your trust, but I opened the letter and I saw it is blank, empty! Jonah, there is no love in that letter!"

Jonah lowered his eyes and caressed his father's letter. After a while, Jonah said, "David, I forgive you. I know you opened it because, like all of us, you are searching for love. You opened the letter and saw nothing because I did not tell you what my father told me. Before I left home, my father said, 'My grandfather taught me a lesson he had heard from his grandfather, a lesson that has been passed down through the generations, a lesson about letters and writing. This lesson teaches us that the letters we write to each other are made of two kinds of fire – black fire and white fire. The letters made of black fire contain the words, and the letters made of white fire contain the spaces between the words and the paper, itself.'

"The end of this ancient teaching is that the white fire is more precious than the black fire. My father explained to me why the blank, white fire letter is more precious. He told me, 'Jonah, the black fire holds the words which describe how much I love you, how much I believe in you and how much I am going to miss you, but Jonah, the white fire is my inability to put into words just how very much I love you. The white fire is like me saying to you, there can never ever be enough words to tell you how much you mean to me; there are just not enough words.' David, my father said to me, 'Here, I am giving you white fire.' Now, you understand, David, the letter is not empty. This letter that my father gave me is filled with White Fire!"

Message

There are times that our love is so heartfelt
that we do not have words to describe it.

Exercise

As we grow up, we wait for someone to share with us those magical words "I love you," and hearing these words has such a healing quality. We are familiar with the importance of learning to verbalize and share our emotions. However, this story focuses on the depth of emotions that we can never express in words. In long-term relationships, a love can develop which is so deep it is beyond words. This explains why people kiss. I kiss you because I do not have enough words to tell you how much I love you. This is also, why people cry at weddings. They are feeling a depth of happiness that cannot be articulated in words. The crying from happiness and the kissing are expressions of the emotions that the story describes as White Fire.

Share this story with your dearest love and then send him or her White Fire – a blank letter.

_____ Affirmation _____

My love for you is so deep, it is beyond words.

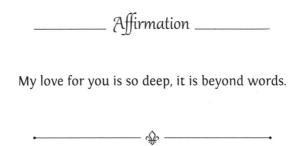

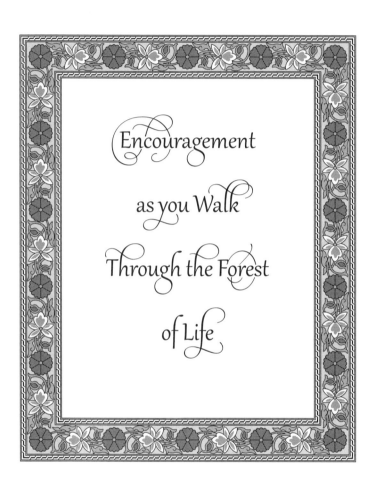

Encouragement

as you Walk

Through the Forest

of Life

The Journey

THERE WERE TIMES when Jonah felt that too many people came to him for advice. Overwhelmed, he would run deep into the forest. There, hidden from probing eyes, he would raise his arms above his head and cry out to God, "God, they ask for advice and they want me to tell them stories, but God, I do not even know what my story is. What is my story?"

Jonah had learned that a conversation with God began with expressing his feelings, but had to continue with sitting and quieting himself. It was in the quiet that he would hear God's messages.

Listening, Jonah wondered,

Was God saying, Be flexible like the swaying branches?

Was God saying, Be soft like the forest floor?

Was God using the wind to breathe new life into him?

Jonah went deeper into his silence and there he found a quiet, calm place. Was God using the trickling water to teach him patience, just as it slowly shaped the stream's pebbles? Was the birds' chirping one of God's ways of helping him find the melodies in his heart? Jonah sat for a long time and allowed his breath to become slow and gentle. In this stillness, a voice awoke inside him, telling him, "Jonah, you are who you are. You are your higher self and you are your lower self. Your story is your journey between these two selves."

––––––––––––––––– Message –––––––––––––––––

All of us have a higher and lower part of ourselves.
Our life story is our journey between the two.

Exercise

Our higher self is all of our positive qualities. Our lower self is all of our negative qualities. List five of your positive and negative qualities. What daily activities are expressions of your positive qualities? What activity would you like to add to either your daily, weekly, or monthly schedule that will help you spend more time with your positive qualities and higher self? What daily activities are expressions of your negative qualities? What would you like to avoid during your daily, weekly, or monthly schedule so as to spend less time with your negative qualities and lower self?

———— Affirmations ————

I enjoy spending time with my higher self.

I admire my higher self.

I comfort and forgive myself after I
spend time with my lower self.

Memories

DAVID WAS A little tired, so instead of chopping, he just sat and watched. He watched the large arc that Jonah's arm created when he raised the axe and was surprised by the immense fury with which Jonah brought his axe crashing down on the large pieces of wood, splintering them into many, many smaller pieces.

After a while, David broke the silence and asked Jonah, "Why are you hitting the wood so hard today?"

Startled by the question, Jonah realized he was smashing his axe against the wood. He stopped and thought about David's query. Finally he explained, "Today I am imagining that each piece of wood is one of my bad memories. When I hit the wood hard, it makes these terrible memories become much smaller."

Intrigued by Jonah's explanation, David asked him, "Does it work?"

"Hmm," Jonah paused to contemplate David's question. "Sometimes yes and sometimes no."

—————————— *Message* ——————————

We have the power to lessen the impact of
negative memories on our present lives.

Exercise

Do you have a bad memory you want to work through?

Begin by writing down the bad memory.

What emotions well up in you when you recall the memory?

How would your life be different if you didn't have that bad memory?

How has this memory held you back from enjoying your life?

Give five answers to the question "If I didn't have this memory I would have. . . ?"

What small changes can you make to live your life as if this bad memory was not a part of you?

Hold a Cleansing Ritual where you take the page with the bad memory and destroy the page by ripping it up, flushing it, etc. As you destroy the paper, say out loud, "I don't want you to be part of my life anymore."

———————— Affirmation ————————

I have the power to lessen the negative
impact of bad memories on my life.

T.T.S.P.

JONAH AND DAVID spent many afternoons together, afternoons filled with raising and lowering their axes. Most of their time was spent in silence. David understood that Jonah liked it that way, but usually could not hold back his questions.

David asked, "Jonah, you said that when you are chopping the wood, you are also making your bad memories smaller. Do you think that would work for me, too?"

"Why you, David?" Jonah asked.

"Because I am all alone and it makes me feel so bad when I remember that I do not have parents."

"David, I too know loneliness," said Jonah, and they continued in silence to chop the wood. When they stopped to rest, Jonah motioned to David to join him and sit on one of the tree stumps. It was then that David noticed the copper ring on Jonah's hand, which bore the inscription: "T.T.S.P."

David asked, "What does T.T.S.P. mean?"

Jonah stared at the ring. It was a while before he answered.

He said, "David, I have experienced great joy and great sadness in my life. Many times, this inscription on my ring, T.T.S.P, has given me comfort. The inscription comes from a very old story. The story is of a king who instructed his most trusted adviser to find him a very special ring, a ring that could bring, at once, ultimate joy and ultimate sadness. The adviser searched and found many rings, from the most ornate to the very simple, but none that were able to invoke both elation and sorrow at the very same time.

"After a while, the adviser heard about a sage, in a far-off province who was also a jeweler. The adviser commissioned this jeweler to make a ring exactly the way the king had instructed him. The adviser examined the finished ring and realized that, at last, he had found exactly what the king was looking for. When the adviser presented the ring to his king, the king began to cry tears of sadness and to laugh with joy. Later, as the king pondered his kingdom and its issues, he would look down at his plain ring and smile when he read its inscription: T.T.S.P. – This Too Shall Pass.

"David, you should know that this is also true for every emotion we experience, like the loneliness you feel in your heart," Jonah explained. "You see, David, these feelings of loneliness that you experience, will also pass. Meanwhile we can chop wood together."

———— *Message* ————
All pain and troubles pass, sooner or later.

Exercise

When we are uncomfortable or in pain, we tend to obsess. We say to ourselves "When will this pass? This will never go away." Then we begin to blame ourselves, "It is my fault I am in pain." And then begin the negotiations. For example: "If the pain goes away, I will never eat X again." Also, when in pain we suddenly discover God: "Oh God, if you just get me through this, I promise I will. . ."

In this story, an important life lesson is presented. When in pain or in a difficult situation, realize it will pass. Then repeat to yourself: "This too shall pass," and notice the positive change in yourself during and after the repetition.

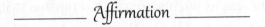

Affirmation

I know that nothing stays the same,
and my pain shall pass, too.

(This advice should be disregarded in the case of an abusive relationship, and does not preclude one from seeking professional, physiological, or physical care.)

The Pouring

I T WAS A hot day for chopping and David was really happy that they took a lot of water breaks. As Jonah dipped the ladle into the water bucket and poured, David said, "Jonah I have been thinking about my parents."

Jonah asked "What have you been thinking?"

"Well, you know I was in the room when my mother was close to dying. They told me to sit on a stool by the dresser, to be very quiet and pray. Do you know what I saw? I saw my mother. She was very white, like there was almost no blood in her face, and she was breathing very slowly. I could see her chest move up and a down a little. Then her chest stopped moving. Grandma Rachel put her hand next to my mother's mouth and nose. Grandma Rachel looked up from my mother and I could tell from her expression that my mother was gone. Jonah, what happened to my mother when she died?"

Jonah once again dipped the ladle and said, "David, when we are born, God pours our soul into us." Then Jonah slowly poured the water back into the bucket. "When we die, God pours our soul back. Your mother stopped breathing because her soul left her body to go back to God. This is why breathing is so important, for with every breath we take, we are breathing in the soul that God is pouring into our body."

—————— *Message* ——————

Breathing connects us to Spirituality.

Exercise

Experiment with this visualization. Find a quiet place. Sit comfortably, close your eyes, breathe, and imagine that God is pouring your soul into you. What emotions are you feeling as you imagine God breathing into you?

You may decide to initiate a conversation with God during this visualization.

————— *Affirmations* —————

God is breathing life into me.

God is breathing encouragement into me.

God's exhale is my inhale.

A Mother's Heart

THEY CONTINUED CHOPPING. After a while David asked "What does it feel like living with God?"

"I don't know if anyone can know. But do you remember when Sarah came over? She asked about your parents. You told her you were an orphan, and then she told us that she was adopted."

"Yes. I remember, but she said she didn't mind being adopted."

"True, but do you remember why she said that?"

"No, not really."

"Well, she said that her mother told her that most mothers carry their babies in their stomachs for nine months, but her mother had carried her in her heart for two years as she waited for the adoption. I think living with God is like living in your mother's heart."

———— Message ————

God as a mother loves us dearly
and holds us in Her heart.

Exercise

In many traditions God is nurturing, comforting, and loving as a mother is.

As our God-concept is initially created from how we view our parents, when we depict God as a mother, we are actually depicting how our mother did or did not love us.

Write down how your mother expressed her love for you as a child and how she is doing so today.

Now write how God as a mother expresses Her love for you. Notice the similarities and differences.

Experiment with perceiving God as a mother.

Affirmations

God holds me like a mother holds her newborn.

God nurtures me.

Clean Water

IT WAS GETTING near suppertime, so Jonah laid his axe down and walked over to the basin to wash his hands. David stood there watching him. He asked, "Jonah, why do you raise your hands to Heaven after you wash them?"

"The answer is a beautiful, yet sad story. Do you want to hear it?"

"You know I do!"

"Do you remember Grandma Rachel?"

David replied, "Yes, of course. She was like a grandma to everyone."

"Yes, she certainly was a very special lady. Towards the end, when she could no longer get out of bed, I used to go visit her and tell her stories. The night that she passed away, she called me. The doctor said that she did not have much time. I sat with her, holding her hand. After a while, she asked for a little water. I could see that her lips were parched so I brought the cup of water to her lips. She looked at me and quietly said, 'No, not to drink. It is for my hands. I want to leave this world with clean hands.' I dipped her hands in the water, she raised them, lowered them, and she passed on. I too, David, hope always to have clean hands."

Message

*Raising our hands to Heaven reminds
us to do good with our hands*

Exercise

Which of your actions cleanse your hands? Which sully
them?

Make up a specific time when your hands will be engaged
in actions that cleanse them.

Say out loud, "For the next hour I will not sully my hands."

Try not to spend time thinking about your failures. Just
keep trying to keep your hands clean.

Affirmations

I am focused on doing good.

When I do good, I feel great.

Fixing Your Life

SIMON WAS THE village banker. He came to see Jonah and pleaded with him, "Jonah, I am so upset. I have made such a mess of my life. Please, Jonah, help me to fix my life."

"Simon, this is a very big request," answered Jonah, "I will need time to think about it. In the meantime, why don't you come inside and help me wash the dishes." They washed dishes in silence for about five minutes. When they were almost finished, Jonah lifted up a freshly washed plate and remarked, "My kindergarten teacher taught me to clean up my own mess. If you have made a mess of your life and feel you can't clean it up, then start by cleaning up your house. Don't let your maid do it – *you* do it because cleaning is cleaning. Once you have practiced cleaning up your house, you will feel more confident about fixing your life."

———— *Message* ————

No matter how many times I repeat
a mistake, I can cleanse myself.

Exercise

To be human is to err, yet the human tragedy is that we repeat our mistakes to the extent that we feel soiled by them. At times, we even lose hope that we can ever be different. If you feel you have soiled yourself because of a weakness or a mistake, there is little point in obsessing about what you have done. Rather, clean yourself up, make amends if needed, and commit yourself to better behavior in the future.

Our focus becomes: from where can one derive the strength to go forward and feel clean once again?

Here are a few possibilities:

Contact a person upon whom you can rely for a friendly word or a positive spin on life.

Take a shower, clean up your room, neaten your house, garage and/or garden.

External cleanliness can give you the strength to clean up your internal emotional dirt.

Eat only healthy food for half a day or even a whole day.

Go for a brisk walk. The physical activity changes the energy, and although the exercise will not change your weakness, it will hopefully give you the strength to go on.

Revisit one of your own previous successes.

Go to a place of beauty to remind yourself that there is
beauty both outside and inside of you.

Ask God to help you. God, by definition, can do anything, and
can therefore give hope in seemingly hopeless situations.

_____ *Affirmation* _____

Fixing smaller issues in my life gives me the
confidence to fix the larger issues.

Holy Thieves

LEAH CAME RUNNING to Jonah, yelling, "Jonah, you must come quickly. My daughter, Debra, is sick. You must heal her!"

"But, Leah, I do not have the power to heal. I am just a simple woodsman."

"But, Jonah, the way people talk about you, you must be close to God. Please come, see my daughter, and pray for her!"

Jonah placed his axe in the shed, put on his jacket, and followed Leah to her cabin. Jonah sat with Debra and prayed, but to no avail. Finally, Jonah asked all the people of the village to assemble, and he announced to them that he would select ten people to pray for Debra. Jonah chose ten people and led them into the forest to pray for Leah's daughter. Some of the village people sneered behind Jonah's back, "What nerve! I always knew he was no good! He chose people of his own kind like Dan the thief, Peter the cheater, and Joe the swindler. Not one honest person among the ten!"

The ten chosen people returned the following morning to find Debra sitting up, sipping teaspoons of soup. The Village Elder asked Jonah, "Why did you choose those ten people?"

Sheepishly Jonah said, "I felt that the Gates of Heaven were locked, so I needed people who would know how to cheat their way into Heaven!"

———— *Message* ————

Sometimes you can learn a critical
life skill from a negative quality.

Exercise

We instruct our children and ourselves to stay away from the con-artist and the cheater, but when correctly channeled, we can find a positive use for even negative qualities.

Write down one of your negative qualities. Think about how it can be used in a positive fashion.

For example:

Use your anger to speak out about or take action against injustice in your community or in the world.

Use your envy of people to motivate you to become wiser or kinder.

Use your pride to realize how much people need self-respect.

Use your high opinion of yourself to realize how important it is to give people confidence in themselves.

Use your carefree attitude towards money to give large amounts to charity (without endangering your financial stability).

Use your ability to lie in order to protect someone else's feelings.

Affirmation

I can use my negative qualities in a positive manner.

Alone?

ON THE EVE of the new month, David went to Jonah's cabin to see how Jonah recited the prayer for the new moon. David had never visited at night and was unsure of how Jonah would welcome his visit, so he hid behind some bushes and watched.

David saw Jonah came out of his cabin. He stood in the clearing, took off his shoes, and rubbed his toes in the grass. Then Jonah spread his arms wide, almost as if he was testing the winds to see if he could fly. Jonah leaned back and swayed from side to side, while reciting the ancient words of thanks to the moon for lighting up the night.

When Jonah was finished, David couldn't control himself, came out from behind the trees and asked Jonah, "Why did you recite the prayer all alone and not with the rest of the village?"

Jonah answered David with a question: "Who was alone?"

——————— Message ———————

When we are in nature or talking
to God, we do not feel lonely.

Exercise

There is a difference between feeling lonely and being alone.

Feeling lonely is a bummer. With no one around, Jonah was without people, yet he felt surrounded by God and nature.

Where can you go where will you be without people, yet not feel alone?

Alternatively, if you can't go to a particular place to be alone, allow yourself to close your eyes for a few minutes and imagine that special place. In your mind, paint your place. Give it colors, dimensions, smells, and feelings.

When you get to such a place, allow yourself to write down your thoughts.

Affirmation

Being in nature nurtures me.

Seeing in the Dark

D AVID ASKED, "WHAT did you pray for?"
Jonah pointed to the moon and said, "For light – the light to brighten people's lives when darkness surrounds them."

"Jonah, I also want to help brighten other people's lives. Maybe that will help take away the loneliness I feel. Can you teach me your prayer for light?"

"Yes, I can. Meet me tomorrow at the edge of the forest at sundown."

Jonah and David met the following evening. As they were about to enter the forest, David went to light his lantern. "No lanterns, David," said Jonah.

"Why not?" asked David. "How will we see our way?"

Jonah answered, "If we cannot see the way in our own darkness, how can we help others to see the way in their darkness?"

—————— *Message* ——————

*We need to work through our own issues
in order to better help others.*

Exercise

The flaws we see in others tend to be the flaws we have inside of ourselves.

For example, a person may be morally demanding on others because they are compensating for some secret immorality. Likewise, a person might be very precise about deadlines or office regulations because they are reacting to disarray experienced in some private areas of life.

Write down the flaws you see in others and then turn your focus on yourself. Realize that you may have a similar flaw in some aspect of your life. Write down or ask your friends how you can sort out these flaws in your own life.

_____ Affirmation _____

I am ready to work through my issues.

———————— ⚜ ————————

The Forest Walk

AFTER SPENDING SO much time with Jonah, David finally felt he was ready. He told Jonah, "I think I am ready to join you when you meditate in the forest."

Jonah asked David, "Do you know what the goal of meditation is?"

"Yes," David replied, "To hear the voice of God."

"Good, David. Then tonight we will go for a walk in the forest."

When it became dark, David joined Jonah at the edge of the forest. David was very surprised when, instead of going deep into the forest, Jonah led them to a spot still within earshot of the village. David remarked, "Jonah, I do not think this is a very good spot to meditate, we can still hear the noises from the village."

Jonah just smiled and sat down in silence. They sat there for a long time, but David could not find the quiet he was seeking. When the meditation was over, Jonah cleared his throat, opened his eyes, and asked, "David, did you hear the voice of God?"

Frustrated, David retorted, "I told you, Jonah, we needed a quieter place, not in earshot of the village. Between hearing Leah's baby crying and the Greensteins' arguing, how could I possibly pay attention to the voice of God?"

Jonah replied, "The more we meditate and concentrate on listening for the voice of God, David, the more motivated we are to open our ears to the crying of babies and to the difficulties that couples go through. What is our purpose and what are we here for, if not to soothe the tears of God's children?"

─────── Message ───────

*Successful meditation leads to being
involved with other peoples' difficulties.*

Exercise

When you embark in meditative practice, ask yourself:
Why do I want to meditate?
What am I expecting to happen?
What benefits am I looking for?

Many people would answer relaxation, peacefulness, clarity in my life, or the settling of one's emotions. Many people report that in establishing a long-term meditative practice, they feel less confused, more focused, and have more control over their emotions and thoughts.

This story presents a different goal for meditation. The

goal here is to find the fortitude to be with other people's pain. The story suggests that the criterion to measure the success of a meditative practice is the degree to which you are involved in other people's difficulties. As you meditate, do not hide from this pain.

Follow the following equation:

$$M = H$$

M = meditation
H = help others

The equation means: The amount of time you spend meditating should equal the amount of time you spend helping others.

———— Affirmation ————

I have the strength to be with other people's pain.

The Two Watchmen

WHEN THE MEDITATION was over, Jonah and David stood up and entered the forest. After a while the canopy was so dense it completely blotted out the moonlight. Standing there in the pitch black darkness of the forest, David asked, "Jonah, you said that you pray for the light to brighten people's lives when darkness surrounds them. But if life did not become dark, there would be no reason to gain the wisdom needed to help people brighten their lives. Jonah, tell me, why does life lose its light?"

Jonah answered David's question with a story about two night watchmen. "Both watchmen held lanterns as they each protected a gate of the village. One day, the Elders of the village approached one of the watchmen and told him, "We no longer have enough money to pay for two lanterns, so we have decided to take your lantern away. The watchman became extremely anxious. He thought to himself, 'How can I continue to do my job with no lantern?'

"Six months went by and the Elders returned. This time they took the lantern away from the second watchman. He too became very troubled – how he was going to do his job properly? Yet the first watchman was not worried anymore because in the six months that had passed without his lantern, he had learned how to see in the dark."

—————— *Message* ——————

*Sometimes we lose our light in order
to learn how to see in the dark.*

Exercise

The same misfortune befalls two people and each grows differently from the misfortune.

Misfortunes are misfortunes. There is no way to change what has happened, but what I can do is ask myself: what can I learn from my misfortune? This is what the story means when it says "Learn how to see in the dark."

The word illumination means both light and understanding because when I understand, I have light.

Make a list of all your misfortunes and explain what you have learned from them.

For example:

Misfortune	What I learned
My parents didn't support me	I learned how to be independent and how critical support is
I had emotional difficulties	I learned how to be emotionally stronger
I was/am financially challenged	I learned how to be happy with less.
	I learned how to focus on the essential qualities of life that create happiness.

This poem from an anonymous author shares a similar sentiment:

I asked for strength
And God gave me difficulties to make me strong.
I asked for wisdom
And God gave me problems to solve.
I asked for prosperity
And God gave me brawn and brain to work.
I asked for courage
And God gave me danger to overcome.
I asked for love
And God gave me troubled people to help.
I asked for favors
And God gave me opportunities.
I ask for my prayers to be answered
And God challenged me to become who I needed to become.
I received nothing I wanted
Yet I received everything I needed.

Affirmations

I have the strength to learn the lessons that
my darkness has come to teach me.

I can see the light in my darkness.

Eating Light

JONAH AND DAVID approached the edge of the forest, where the village began. "Jonah, before we end our walk, please explain to me, how do you bring light to someone?"

"It is very late, David. Let it go for now. Tomorrow is a new day."

"No, Jonah, now. Please tell me now, before we reach the end of the forest."

"All right, David, I will explain with a funny story and maybe in this story you will find an answer to your question."

Jonah continued, "Grandma Rachel did not have any grandchildren and I did not have a grandmother, so we decided to adopt each other. I would visit her once a week for a grand meal of chicken soup, chicken, potatoes, sour pickles, and sugar cookies. Sadly, in time, she became so frail that our visits became just tea and cookies."

"One day," Jonah went on, "she said to me, 'Jonah, I do not have the strength to make you a meal, but I really miss my own cooking, and nothing would make me happier than to have some good food.' So I went home and cooked. I did my best and came back with chicken soup, chicken, and potatoes.

"When I walked into her cabin, she laughed and said, 'I could smell you coming!' I laid all the food out on the table and she said to me, 'Jonah, you have made me so happy.' We sat for a few moments staring at all the food. Food had been such a big part of our connection and I waited for her to start eating, but she didn't. Finally, I said to her, 'I thought you wanted to eat?'

Jonah reflected and went on with the story, "'Oh,' she said, 'I am not hungry.' I was surprised at her reply and asked her why she wanted me to bring her food and she said, 'Because nothing would make me happier than watching you eat the food.' So, David, you see, I ate and in this way I brought her light."

Message

*Responding to other people's
needs brings them light.*

Exercise

Usually, we bring light into people's lives by doing something altruistic. The unique form of bringing light found in this story is through receiving and not giving. It is Jonah and not the Grandmother, who eats.

For example:

I allow someone to give me a present or do me a favor that I really do not need. This brings light because the giver now feels important and useful.

I listen to a person share a story or information which I have already heard. This brings them light because I am giving them your attention that they so desperately seek.

_____ *Affirmation* _____

I can bring light into people's lives.

————————— ⚜ —————————

The Walk

THE VILLAGE ELDER went to Jonah. "Jonah, so many people flock to you to hear your wisdom. I want to know, how did you gather so much wisdom?"

Jonah politely smiled and remained silent.

The Elder pressed on, "Jonah, before your life fell apart, were you an Elder?"

Jonah shook his head no.

"A teacher?" asked the Elder, and again, Jonah shook his head no.

"A university professor?"

Jonah's reaction was again no.

"Jonah, tell me, what is the source of your profound wisdom?"

At last, Jonah answered the Elder, "The source is the walks. Walking in the forest reminds me that we are always on a journey, a journey that asks two questions of us: Who are we and why are we here? What I share with everyone, are the answers I hear while I am walking."

—————— Message ——————

Life is a constant journey of exploration through introspection

Exercise

Make walking a part of your daily routine.

As you walk, ask yourself, "Who am I and why am I here?"

After the walk, write down your answers.

By doing so, you will be enrolling yourself into your own school of exploration and introspection.

As you walk, ask yourself questions about what is troubling you, and you will discover an inner guide that will reveal and share answers.

_____ Affirmations _____

Walking frees my mind.

I think deeply when I walk.

Walking helps me answer the questions:
"Who am I and why am I here?

Disappearing Kites

SARAH WAS A young girl from the village school. She came to see Jonah and asked him, "Why do you believe in God, Jonah?"

Jonah looked down at the pile of wood in front of him and thought that he had done enough. Jonah said, "Time to take a break. Do you like flying kites?"

Sarah's face lit up. "I really do!" she exclaimed.

Jonah smiled and said, "I do, too. Let us go fly our kites!"

Sarah ran home and brought her kite. The kite was almost as tall as she was, with bright red cloth spread over a wooden frame. Sarah saw that Jonah also had a kite. Jonah's kite was smaller than her kite, and it was light blue like the sky. Jonah led her into a clearing where they let out their kites. Jonah suggested to Sarah, "With such a strong wind, we can free our kites even more!" So, they did.

Sarah asked, "Jonah, more?"

"Sure," he replied, "The wind is strong enough!" The kites began to climb higher and higher into the sky. Sarah's red kite was seen for miles around, but Jonah's blue kite seemed to disappear against the blue sky.

Sarah said, "Jonah, I can barely see your kite. How do you know it is still there?"

Jonah replied, "Because I can feel the kite tugging me.

And that is why I believe in God, because I feel God tugging at me."

———— *Message* ————

There are moments when we feel
God tugging at our heart.

Exercise

What can help us feel God tugging at our hearts?
- Find a quiet place in nature and listen.
- Visit a hospital's baby nursery.
- Hold your own baby or a friend's baby.
- Listen to or sing along with children.

———— *Affirmation* ————

I enjoy feeling God tugging at my heart.

God Water

SARAH HAD REALLY enjoyed flying kites together with Jonah. She visited Jonah again because she had some more questions. Sarah needed an explanation. "Jonah, I want to make sure I understand. When we flew our kites, you said you believe in God because you feel God tugging at you, like your kite."

Jonah smiled and made a tugging motion in the air. Sarah continued, "But can you explain to me what God is?"

Jonah said, "Sarah, you are so young, yet so deep. Let us go for a walk to the river." Sarah had been to the river a thousand times, yet this time she knew it would be different. Jonah asked Sarah to kneel down and look into the water. They saw two orange fish swimming near the bank of the river. Kneeling together on the bank, Jonah asked, "Sarah, can you ask your question again?"

"Sure, can you explain what God is?"

Jonah explained, "The answer to your question is here in the water. Imagine that the two fish you see in the river are talking to each other and one fish is asking the other fish, 'What is this thing called water?'"

"Sarah, just like a fish explains what water is, that is how I explain what God is."

————————— *Message* —————————

God surrounds us and lives inside us just as
water surrounds and lives inside fish.

————————————————————

Exercise

God, by definition, is everywhere. Everywhere means outside
and inside of us, just like water which surrounds and flows
through fish.

Why does God want to surround us and live inside us?
Because God wants to have an intimate relationship with
each one of his children, no matter their race, gender, reli-
gion, size, color, or shape. All humans yearn to not be lonely.
Our loneliness is lightened when we are in a relationship in
which there is deep sharing of emotions and interests. In
these relationships we experience a oneness similar to the
intimacy Gods wants to have with us – inside and surround-
ing us. The exercise is to ask myself to what degree do I want
to be one with God? In what areas of my life do I want to
invite God to enter? How would my life be different if I was
becoming closer to God? And, if I desire to come closer to
God, what is holding me back from doing so?

———————Affirmations———————

Enveloped in water, I experience being one with God.

God wants to be intimate with me.

The Teacher

A SEMINARY STUDENT TOLD Jonah, "Jonah, I am searching for a teacher who will teach me about God."

Jonah said, "Sit here on this stump and I will tell you a story. Once a student had an interview with the head teacher so he could join the finest seminary in Europe. The head teacher told the student, 'This interview is based on your answer to one question only, why did you choose to come here?'

"The student did not hesitate and answered the head teacher directly, 'To find God.'

"The teacher said, 'Go home. God is everywhere.' The student realized his chances of being accepted were crumbling, so he quickly responded, 'But I thought you help people find God.'

"The head teacher told the student, 'No, I help people find themselves.' Seeing the confusion on the student's face, the head teacher added, 'God created you because God wants to have a relationship with you, but if you do not know yourself, then with whom is God going to have a relationship?'"

——————— *Message* ———————

*God created you because God wants to
have a relationship with you, but if you
do not know yourself, then with whom
is God going to have a relationship?*

——————————————————

Exercise

There are billions of people in the world, so what was God's need to create me? In God's infinite wisdom, the answer is already known. The pathway for us finite humans to answer the question "Why did God create me?" is through self-discovery. The more we discover how we are uniquely different from everyone else, the closer we come to God's goal in creating the individual self.

The simple, but difficult path to discovering God's need for me is by discovering my strengths and activating them in the service of God. The definition of serving God is using my strength for the betterment of humanity.

The exercise is to list your strengths and create a plan how you can use each strength to better yourself and others.

For example:

My Strength	How to use my strength for the improvement of people's lives
Physically strong	Help carry needy people or their belongings. Participate in a walkathon and get sponsors.
Patient	Teach others how to manage their anger.
Understanding	Listen to people's problems/issues.
Detail-oriented	Help a friend/family member workout a plan to straighten out their finances or apply for jobs/schools. Do medical, social or environmental research.
Musical	Write songs that inspire people. Sing or play for people in need, or to cheer up a friend.

_____ *Affirmations* _____

Knowing that God wants to have a relationship
with me makes me feel happy and cared for.

The more I know myself, the more
I know God's need for me.

Answered Prayers

"I PRAY AND PRAY, but nothing happens," David complained.

"I am sure God listens to your prayers," Jonah replied. "I think God listens to my prayers, and God also listens to your prayers, too."

David pressed on, "If God listens, then why doesn't God answer?"

Jonah said, "You know, David, I once asked my mother the same question and she answered me with a story."

Jonah began to tell his story, "Once when my mother passed by my sister Hannah's room, she saw that Hannah's doll had come apart. My mother asked Hannah, 'What are you going to do?' and Hannah replied, 'I am going to pray.'

"A few hours later, when my mother saw that the doll was still in pieces, she approached Hannah, asking her, 'Did you pray?'

"Hannah answered, 'Yes, I did.'

"'I guess God did not answer your prayer,' my mother remarked to Hannah.

"'Oh, no, Mom,' Hannah replied, 'God did answer my prayer, but God's answer was no.'

"So, you see, David, God answers, yet sometimes God's answer is no."

_____ Message _____

Sometimes God says no.

Exercise

When does God hear our prayers? Immediately! However, God knows how our prayers need to be answered. Sometimes God says no because God has our best interests at heart, even though we do not understand why life is treating us with discomfort or worse.

Sometimes prayers are not answered because it is not the right time. We have our schedule and God has God's schedule. They do not always coincide.

Sometimes prayers are not answered because God wants to make sure that we really want or need what we are praying for. Alternatively, God knows when this is not the right time for God's intervention, but rather the time for us to become active and change our lives. This is similar to when we knock on a locked door and the door does not open. The door may be saying, "Knock harder," because the door wants to make sure we really want to get inside. However, the door may be saying "I am not opening up to you because your answer lies elsewhere."

When God is ready to answer, but God wonders if we really want what we are praying for

There are times when God decides that God is going to answer our prayers immediately. However, God wants to be certain we are ready to have our prayers answered. Then, to have our prayers answered, we need to make sure we really want what we are praying for. This can be accomplished by praying for the same thing over and over again, preferably, on a daily basis, for weeks on end. After praying for the same thing repeatedly, hopefully, God will agree that we are ready to receive the answer to our prayers.

You may develop this type of steadfastness by planting a seed in a pot or in the ground. Take a few moments each day and stand by your covered seed, yearning for it to break through the soil, and carefully nourishing the seed with water and fertilizer until it flourishes. Is this not what we are going through?

When God wants to say yes, but we are not yet worthy to receive

When God has decided we are not yet ready to receive our requested answer, we need to make ourselves ready. If God has said no because God has decided we are not yet ready to receive, then the following writing exercise can help move us forward.

Writing exercise:

What can I do to become worthy of God's positive answer?

What changes do I need to make in my physical life, emotional life, and relationship life?

What do I need to learn to become worthy of receiving that which I need from God?

What efforts do I need to make so God will deem me ready?

_____Affirmations_____

I am ready to have my prayers answered.

My actions bring me closer to that which I pray for.

There Is a Reason for Pain

THE VILLAGE ELDER sat with Jonah and said, "Jonah, I have listened to your stories and it is clear to me that you have gathered great wisdom from many of your life's experiences. I believe that many of your experiences were not only unpleasant, but very painful as well. I know it is written that 'A gem is not polished without rubbing, nor a man perfected without trials.' But it still hurts."

Jonah shared a sad, knowing smile with the Elder.

"Pain, Jonah. There is so much pain. People come to me and share their hardships, their brokenness. Jonah, what do you advise? What should I tell them in their pain?"

Jonah closed his eyes, rocking his head back and forth and finally said, "I don't know." The Elder waited. Jonah stared at his hands. "Maybe it would be enough to just hold their hands," he reflected. The Elder waited, quietly.

Then Jonah remembered and said, "There is a story of a man who rented his fields from a nobleman. They had an honorable relationship, but at the end of the year, the nobleman left, leaving his affairs in the hands of his brother. The brother summoned the man and said, 'Things were too easy for you until now. I am going to raise your rent by twenty percent and you have three weeks to pay me. And for every day that you are late in paying me, you will get ten lashes!' The man rushed out and scrounged, borrowed and begged. Luckily, he was able to put together all the money. The nobleman's brother said, 'Sure enough, you have brought me all the money, but you are three days late.' The man was tied to a tree and given thirty lashes. When he returned home, his wife saw him and cried, 'What happened, why you are so sad?' The man told his wife what had happened."

Jonah continued, "At the end of the year, the nobleman returned and heard what his brother had done in his absence. He summoned the man and said to him, 'I heard what happened to you and I am very sorry. First of all, my brother is going to give you back the extra twenty percent and, second, he is going to give you ten rubles for every lash you received.' The man looked at the three hundred rubles being placed on the table. It was a small fortune. When he arrived home, his wife saw him and once again she cried, 'What happened to you, why are you so sad? Did they thrash you again?' The man answered his wife, 'No, they did not, but I wish I would have gotten more lashes.'"

———— *Message* ————

*There are times when our condition
improves only through pain.*

Exercise

This story captures the terrible aspect of our reality, that there are times when our betterment can only come through experiencing physical or emotional difficulties.

In the world of nature, we recognize this process as we witness:

Grapes being crushed so they can become champagne.
Olives being pressed so they can produce healthy, life-giving oil.
Bread molding so it can save lives in the form of penicillin.
Milk souring so it can transform into cheese.
Cataclysmic pressures pressing coal into diamonds.

This process of betterment through pain is well known by athletes or by students who welcome harsh criticism in order to improve their performance.

Unfortunately, improvement through pain is also well known by those of us who have undergone chemotherapy. Let us pray that a non-painful treatment can be found to fight disease. In the meantime, it is crucial to find people whom you love and trust, who can hold your hand during such difficult journeys.

Visualization

Choose one of the examples from the world of nature: grapes, olives, bread, or coal. Sit in a quiet place. Close your eyes. Imagine that you are a grape, olive, etc., being placed in a vise. You feel the pressure, you feel the pain, and it is difficult to be in this situation. Slowly, ever so slowly, you see yourself being transformed from a grape into liquid champagne.

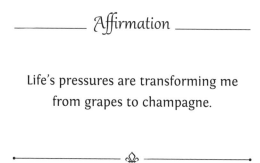

——————— *Affirmation* ———————

Life's pressures are transforming me
from grapes to champagne.

Who Is Plowing What?

THE ELDER THOUGHT about life's lashes and their promise of being transformed into a reward. Finally he said, "Jonah, that is such a harsh answer. People come to me for hope. I ask of you, Jonah, please tell me a story filled with hope."

Jonah thought about his own lashes and looked at the Elder with tears in his eyes. The Elder was not satisfied; he needed more from Jonah. He prodded him, "What about you, Jonah? What about your pain? What gives you hope?"

Jonah answered the Elder, "When I was young, the Tsar's soldiers came and took my grandfather away. The story goes that he was speaking against the Tsar in public. I remember my grandmother was so worried because with grandfather gone, there would be no one to plow the potato fields. I sat by her while she wrote a letter to my grandfather, sharing her worries and explaining how she would have to hire help to plow the fields.

"Almost like a miracle, she got a reply from my grandfather, all the way from Siberia. Yet I can still feel her fear, inside of me, when she read my grandfather's letter to the family. My grandfather wrote, 'Do not plow the potato fields because that is where I buried all the letters against the Tsar.'

"The fear became a reality when, a week later, she came running to our cabin, yelling, 'The soldiers, the soldiers are here, they must have read the letter, they are digging up all the potato fields!' We were very thankful to God, when the Tsar's soldiers did not find anything and she wrote to my grandfather to let him know.

"Grandfather wrote back, saying, 'Now, you can sow the potato fields!'"

─────────── *Message* ───────────

There are life events that feel like our
fields are being torn apart when, actually,
they are being prepared for sowing.

─────────────────────────

Exercise

Make a list of people or events that, intentionally or unintentionally, harmed or nearly harmed you and yet these events helped you to better your life.

For Example:

You were fired, only to find a better job.

A business deal failed, only to save you even greater financial loss.

A relationship soured, so you could find true love.

Affirmations

I know life is preparing me for sowing, even though it feels like I am being torn apart.

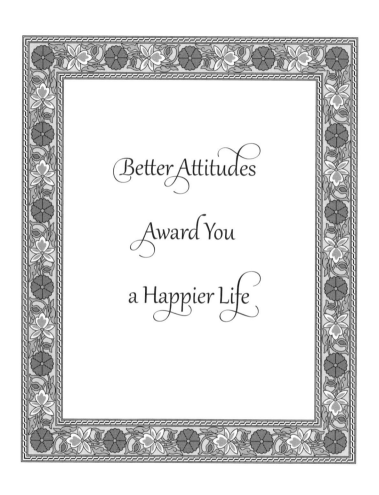

Better Attitudes

Award You

a Happier Life

Quenching Thirst

AT TIMES DAVID would just sit on a log and watch Jonah in the silence. David watched while Jonah worked and watched Jonah when he took his breaks. At first David thought Jonah took breaks to rest, but when Jonah stopped working, instead of closing his eyes, he would fix his eyes on something in the distance and would breathe deeply. What interested David even more was the smile that would form on Jonah's face as he sat, fixated.

Finally David asked, "Jonah, what do you do during your breaks?"

"I rest," Jonah replied.

"But, Jonah, when you rest you don't close your eyes, you just sit there smiling!"

Jonah explained, "Sitting is like drinking water. Imagine dipping a glass into the river. The water in the glass is cloudy at first, but if you set the glass down and let the water settle, the water becomes clear and you can then drink the water. When I sit, my mind settles and becomes clear just like the water in the glass. This is when I feel rested and at peace."

Message

*Relaxation comes when we learn
how to settle our minds.*

Exercise

List three places that calm your mind.

List three activities that calm your mind.

Once a week, go to a place and do one of the activities that
calms your mind.

Every day, spend between five to fifteen minutes in silence.

When you finish, write down your thoughts.

When most people begin to relax, they feel agitated with
the silence because in the silence they begin to hear what
their mind, heart, or soul needs to share, yet they are not
ready to listen to them. However, with practice, they learn
to welcome and love the silence.

Ask yourself what it is about the silence that agitates you.

After practicing, ask yourself what you have come to like
about being silent.

Affirmation

I enjoy having a settled mind.

The Vest

DAVID ASKED, "JONAH, why do you always wear a vest?"

Jonah answered, "David, my vest has two pockets, one on either side of my vest. In each pocket, I have placed a little note. One note says, 'The world was created for me' and the other note says, 'I am but the dust of the earth.'"

Jonah explained, "You see, David, I live my life in a balance between these two notes."

——————— Message ———————

Life is the balance between feeling full
of our strengths and having the humility
to use these strengths wisely.

———————————————

Exercise

Humility comes when we realize that there is more to our life than satisfying our own myriad of personal desires, that we are part of a bigger picture, which may be a relationship, family, community, nation, or universe.

Some think that humility is equal to meekness, but really

humility equals self-knowledge, i.e., the knowledge of my strengths and weaknesses. Humility comes to temper our strengths, so that instead of being full of ourselves, we use our strengths for the greater good.

Make a list of ten of your strengths. List how you can selflessly use each one of your strengths. Choose one action from your list. Do it during the upcoming week.

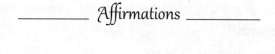

Affirmations

I know my strengths.

I enjoy using my strengths for the greater good.

How Big Are Your Hands?

ELI TOOK OFF his apron, hung it on the wall, and closed his store. "I really need to talk to Jonah," he said to himself and went directly to the edge of the village, where he found Jonah chopping wood.

"Hello Eli. How is the store doing?" Jonah inquired.

"Don't ask – I have too many problems. Between running the store, my kids, and weather-proofing my cabin, I have many, many problems!"

"Well, I was just about to take a break. Would you like to join me for a walk?" So Jonah and Eli went off.

Eli waited for Jonah to say something to ease his burden, but Jonah was silent. He led them to a rise which overlooked the village. Finally Jonah said, "Eli, take a look and tell me what you see."

Eli looked at Jonah and said, "Please, Jonah, no games. I need advice."

All Jonah would say was, "Tell me, Eli, what you see?"

Eli told Jonah what he saw. He described the village, the road running through the village and the forest surrounding the entire village.

"Now, Eli," continued Jonah, "put your hand over your eyes and tell me what you see."

"Please, Jonah, enough is enough! I am a busy man." Yet

Jonah would not relent. Finally, Eli covered his eyes and said, "Fine! Are you happy? I see nothing!"

Jonah then said, "Eli, you are married, you have children and a business. All your problems, I dream of having. Eli, lower your hand and look at it. Just as our hands can blind us from seeing nature's beauty, so too can life's pressures blind us from appreciating the wonder of our lives. Go home, Eli! Go back to your work and uncover your eyes!"

Message

Life's pressures blind us to all that we have.

Exercise

Make a list of everything that is going well in your life.

Write a thank you note to either God, your partner, your children, your friends, your parents, or your fellow employees for everything they have done for you.

Write a note thanking yourself for what you have given to yourself.

Thankfulness helps us see all that we have in our lives.

If you find this exercise challenging, ask yourself why do I choose to focus on my difficulties instead of focusing on what is good and positive in my life?

Remember: darkness cannot be beaten away with a stick, but it can be dispelled by lighting a candle. Bringing yourself down by focusing on the negative is the stick. Thankfulness is lighting the candle.

————— *Affirmations* —————

I allow myself to see my life as it truly is.

I enjoy being thankful.

Needs

FOR A FEW days Eli walked around repeating to himself, "I need to take my hand off my eyes." Finally he found himself back watching Jonah and David having a long and heated conversation which ended with David storming back to the village. Jonah looked at Eli, and in an exasperated voice said, "Children."

Eli smiled when he said, "My turn." Then he began "Jonah, I liked walking with you and I have tried taking your advice, 'To take your hand off your eyes' just like you told me, but it is not working. I am so busy with so much to do! I need to wake up early to have time to say the morning prayers. I have to open the store early enough so people can start their day. I need to be in the store all day to serve everyone. I need to stay late to make sure all the supply books are in order. I need to make enough money for all my kids and I need to spend time with my family. Don't you understand, Jonah? I have too many problems!"

Jonah breathed deeply before replying, trying to let his slow breaths make room for both David's and Eli's complaints.

Finally, he said "What I understand is that you have figured out what you need, but not why you are needed!"

Eli listened. He knew he understood all of Jonah's words

but was trying to piece together the meaning. What did Jonah mean that he knew what he needed but not why he was needed?

Jonah saw Eli's face crease up in deliberation, so he continued.

"Eli, how does it feel to have a needy wife?"

"It is difficult."

"Eli, how does it feel to be needed by your wife?" Eli paused to think about that.

Jonah continued "Eli, how does it feel to have needy children?"

"It tires me out."

"But, Eli, how does it feel to be needed by your children? Doesn't it feel wonderful to come back at the end of the day to a wife and children?"

Jonah paused, looked down the path at David and said, "Needy children may drain us, but doesn't it feel great to be needed by children? Eli, seeing life's demands as needs will eventually drain you. Yet, seeing life's demands as why you are needed will fill your heart with joy.

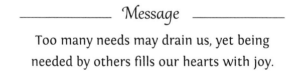

Too many needs may drain us, yet being needed by others fills our hearts with joy.

Exercise

Make a list of all the reasons you are needed by your partner, your children, your parents, your extended family, your friends, your work, your neighborhood, and others. Smile to yourself. Feeling that you are needed in this world is an awesome, invigorating feeling.

Who needs me?	Why do they need me?
Partner	
Children	
Friends	
Parents	

If you feel that you are not needed enough, then offer more of your time to others.

_____ Affirmations _____

I know what I need and I know why I am needed.

Knowing that people need me enriches my life.

How Can I Lighten My Load?

THIS TIME WHEN Eli, the owner of the general store, came back, he found Jonah loading his wheelbarrow with fresh cut timber. "Jonah, I have thought about what you said about needing and being needed, and you know, you are right. It feels so much better understanding that God needs my prayers, that the village people need my services and that I am really needed at home. It makes me feel that I belong to something larger than myself. But still, I get so tired and at times it is so overwhelming. How can I lighten my load?"

"Eli, I could carry this timber over to the cord but instead I put it in the wheelbarrow. Why is that?"

"Because it is easier."

"Yes, but why is it easier?"

"Because the wheelbarrow's slant and wheel carry most of the weight of the wood, and all you have to do is push. Wait a minute, are you hinting that I need something to help me carry the weight that I am carrying?"

"Yes I am," Jonah replied. "Yet let me add something complicated that Zev, the coach driver, once told me. The coach was full so he had the extra passenger sit next to him. Zev noticed that the passenger had a heavy pack on his back. After a while, Zev said to him, 'Why don't you

154 · Jonah the Woodchopper

lighten your load and take your pack off your back?' The passenger said, 'I would, but I do not want my load to be heavy for the horses.'

"Listen, Eli, one of the secrets of life is learning to carry our own loads and to allow the horses to carry what they are already carrying."

———————— *Message* ————————

One of the secrets of life is learning to carry what we must, and to allow God to share the load.

———————————————————

Exercise

The story is a complex metaphor containing inner wisdom that we usually are not taught in school, or even at home. The passenger's heavy pack is a metaphor for life's different responsibilities such as financial and familial responsibilities. The horses are a metaphor for God who is a silent partner in our lives and carries us even if we do not notice His support.

To accomplish our life's purpose, we must become strong enough to carry life's responsibilities. Yet there comes a time when we have to trust and allow our lives to unfold without our active intervention. The passenger has not learned this lesson. Therefore, he continues to carry his pack even though the horses are already carrying it for him.

When life gets too heavy, we can say to God, "God, I have

done my share. Now I give it over to You, for in any event You are always carrying me."

Affirmations

God, I know you support me.

God, I am comforted knowing you are there to support me when my life gets too heavy.

Rock Candy

THE BELL TINKLED when Jonah entered Eli's store. Jonah had a craving for rock candy and the general store was the only place it was sold. Jonah really liked rock candy but felt he had to watch his weight.

"Eli, a pound of rock candy, please. No, make it half a pound," Jonah said as he put a few coins on the counter.

"I am so happy to see you," Eli said as he scooped the rock candy into a paper bag. "Today has been crazy. The new seeds came in and all day people have been placing orders. People, sacks of seeds, new order forms – I am feeling completely overwhelmed. Jonah, give me a few words of encouragement."

"Well, as today is candy day, I will tell you something sweet. A man was walking through the forest when suddenly there was a huge bear in front of him. He ran away but soon realized that he was nearing a cliff. With the bear on his heels he had no option but to jump off. Luckily there were huge tree roots which had broken through the edge of the cliff. He landed on one of these roots and began to climb down. But at the bottom of the cliff was the bear's mate – I guess they were hunting as a team. So the man couldn't climb up or down. Hanging there and trying to figure out what to do, he heard a biting noise. Looking up, he saw that honey had dripped down from a tree onto the roots, and the bear was eating the root he was holding onto."

"Jonah, so far this isn't too encouraging."

"Wait for the end. Looking around, he noticed a berry bush with ripe red berries growing out of the cliff.

"The man ate a berry and said, 'This is a really sweet berry,'" and with that Jonah popped a piece of rock candy into his mouth.

Eli was dumbfounded. "That's it! What happened to the man?"

"He died."

"Died? So what is encouraging about the story?"

Jonah let the sweet flavor of the candy fill his mouth and then said, "With the bear, the cliff, the bear's mate, and his imminent death, the man could still taste the sweetness of the berries. Eli, on hard days, have a piece of candy and taste how sweet life is."

———— *Message* ————

Don't let life's pressures make you
forget how sweet life really is.

Exercise

What is going to be our response when:
- We have a lot to get done
- Life throws us a lot of curveballs
- Life's pressures keep mounting

At times we are going to:

Get a headache, backache, neck ache, stomachache, get depressed and feel lethargic, eat fatty, unhealthy, comfort food, or snap angrily at our loved ones.

In this story there is a very sweet message. When you feel pressured you can respond with a rock candy response, as demonstrated in this chart.

Pressure	Regular response	The Rock Candy response
Have deadlines to meet	Work harder, stress out, eat junk food, get irritable	I take off my shoes midday and massage my feet
		I make sure to leave home with a healthy salad for lunch
		I turn off my cell phone and take ten minutes to listen to my favorite music
		I turn off my cell phone and stare out the window for five minutes
		I close my eyes and think about one person who really believes in me

—————— *Affirmation* ——————

In the face of pressure, I make sure to pamper myself.

Sweet Coffee

ELI CAUGHT UP to Jonah just as he was about to pick up his axe and begin a day of chopping. "Jonah, I have this new kind of coffee. It is imported, all the way from Africa. You have to have a cup with me."

Jonah put down his axe and said, "Eli, I would love to start the day with you and a good cup of coffee."

Jonah watched as Eli put a spoon of sugar and then a spoon of coffee into a small cup, poured the hot water from the kettle, and mixed it. Eli gave the cup to Jonah and said, "Here, Jonah, smell it before you drink it. Isn't it great?"

"Yes, Eli, it sure does smell wonderful!" Jonah exclaimed.

Eli made himself a cup of coffee as well, and sat down next to Jonah on one of the tree stumps. He turned to Jonah saying, "There is nothing like a good cup of coffee to start your day." And he took his first sip. They sat, enjoying the quiet. After a few minutes, Eli noticed that Jonah had not touched his coffee. "Jonah, why aren't you drinking your coffee?"

"Eli, I don't want to hurt your feelings, but you do not know how to make coffee." Eli looked shocked, but waited for Jonah's explanation.

"Eli, I saw you put the sugar in first and then the coffee and that is why I cannot drink the coffee. The sweetness of

160

sugar reminds me to be compassionate while the bitterness of coffee reminds me of how judgmental I can be. When I make coffee, I put the coffee in first and only then, sweeten my judgmental nature with compassion using sugar."

——— *Message* ———

Sweeten your judgmental
nature with compassion.

Exercise

All of humanity is looking for a kind word. If we have decided that it is necessary to say something sharp, we need to sweeten the sharpness with some kindness.

For example:

Before you say something sharp to your partner, pay them a compliment.

Before you give your children a piece of your mind, remind them that you love them.

When you send your child to his or her room for twenty minutes, make it only ten minutes.

When writing an email expressing your displeasure, write it, wait twenty-four hours, and then rewrite it using kinder language.

######### Affirmations #########

I enjoy being sweet.

Being sweet is one of my strengths.

❦

The Honest Non-Thief

"JONAH, I HAVE a confession to make," David began. "I was standing outside the general store just when Eli got a new shipment of boots. There were so many, maybe twenty or even thirty pairs of new boots, all shiny and some even lined with fur. People were picking them up to see how the boots' shine caught the sunlight."

Jonah looked down at David's old battered boots and asked, "So what is your confession?"

"I wanted to take the boots. I had it all planned out. With the ruckus of a new shipment and people admiring the boots, I would also pick up a pair of boots, hold them up to the sun, turn from everyone, and slowly walk away. Eli would assume he got the numbers of the order wrong or demand another pair from the boot seller, but no one would suspect me."

Jonah again looked at David's old boots and asked, "Well you didn't take the boots. So what is your confession?"

"That I wanted to, I really wanted to. I wanted to steal. How can I be an honest person if I want to steal?"

"David, my grandmother taught me that 'A man is not honest simply because he never had a chance to steal. An honest person is one who is tempted to steal but doesn't.'"

Message

When we are tempted, we are given the
opportunity to overcome our urges and show
ourselves how dedicated we are to our values.

Exercise

In the vacuum of space, our muscles atrophy because there is no resistance. Our muscles become strong on Earth because they are working against the Earth's gravitational pull. The same is true with our value muscles. They do not grow in a vacuum. Our value system grows when we are pulled in the opposite direction and yet we work to stay dedicated to our values. Our sports teachers would have said "No pain, No gain."

Make a chart listing the temptations you are resisting or are trying to resist, and the values they come to strengthen.

For example:

Temptation I am resisting or trying to resist	My values that are being strengthened
Theft	Honesty
Adultery	Fidelity
Drugs	Facing up to my reality
Food	Physical health
Selfishness	Giving of yourself
Laziness	Valuing my life

———— *Affirmations* ————

Resisting my temptations makes me a better person.

No pain. No gain.

I am now overcoming my temptations.

———————— ⚜ ————————

Boots

ELI TRIED TO sell Jonah a new pair of boots. "Jonah, I just got in a huge selection of boots. I know you may not have all the money for a new pair of boots, but I am sure we can work something out."

"Sorry, Eli. I am not interested," Jonah replied.

"Jonah, I do not understand. I have been trying to sell you a new pair boots for three years. It is time, Jonah. Your boots are so worn out. They could have even been your father's boots."

"Actually, they were my father's boots."

Not letting anything stop him, Eli continued, "Then, Jonah, it surely is time for a new pair."

"No, Eli, my father gave me his boots," Jonah countered.

Eli realized that Jonah had more to say about his boots and asked, "Jonah, what makes your boots so important to you?"

"These heavy coarse boots belonged to my father. In fact, I never remember them getting a shine. My father would only wear them when it snowed. He was the head of a large seminary. When it snowed, he would put on these boots and walk back and forth, from the seminary dorm to its study hall, until he had cut a path in the snow. He was making sure the boys could walk safely to the study hall to begin their studies."

"Now I understand, Jonah," Eli said. "You wear your father's boots so you, too, can help cut and make pathways for people."

"True," Jonah explained. "Yet actually, I wear these boots so I can feel that I am finding a pathway back to my father."

———————— *Message* ————————

Hold onto objects that connect you to your past.

Exercise

We live in a "throw away" culture. This is true regarding many aspects of our lives for example:

- We throw away plastic dishes, cups, bags, etc.
- We buy shirts that we may wear only once or twice.
- We get toys that we know aren't going to stay whole for very long.

How many of us possess something old like a grandfather's watch or pen.

Or do the following:

- Sleep in your father's shirt.
- Wear your grandmother's apron or use her pots.
- Sit at your parents' dining room table or grandfather's desk.

This exercise begins by asking yourself, "What physical objects connect you to your past?" Ask your parents or grandparents to give you something which will connect you to your past and that you may even pass on to the next generation. As we hold onto these objects we feel rooted. Objects from our past make us feel safe. Although our lives, at times, have a fleeting plastic quality, we can still feel grounded and rooted.

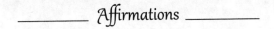

Affirmations

I feel grounded and rooted.

Connecting to my past makes me feel safe.

Connecting to my past makes me feel grounded.

What Do You Smell?

BITING INTO A bright red tomato, Eli said, "This is so sweet. Do you grow your own?"

"No," replied Jonah. "I trade wood for them with Nathaniel, the milkman, who grows them on the other side of the village."

"You know, plenty of people grow their own tomatoes, but these are absolutely beautiful. Maybe I'll start selling them at the store. I wonder how Nathaniel gets them so sweet and juicy."

"This," said Jonah "is a secret, a secret of tomato growing and a secret of life. Do you know why Nathaniel lives way on the other side of the village?"

"Of course. This way the smell from his cows isn't so strong."

"You know, Eli, we smell the stench, but Nathaniel smells fertilizer, and that is why his tomatoes are so good. This is also one of the secrets of life. Life sends us foul-smelling hardships, but it is our job to turn them into fertilizer."

——————— Message ———————

Hardships help you grow – even though
living through hardships is not pleasant

Exercise

Make a list of hardships you experienced. I suggest choosing one period from your life--childhood, the teen years, pre/post-college years, adulthood, marriage, or parenthood. You may want to follow this chart.

For example: Childhood

Hardship	Is wasn't pleas-ant because	The ways it helps me grow
My parents moved all the time	I never felt rooted or a real belonging	I learned how to easily make friends
Absentee parent	I felt alone	Self-sufficiency
My grandparents died when I was twelve	I lost their unconditional love	Taught me how to value family members

───── Affirmation ─────

Hardships are an opportunity for growth.

Angry Pebbles

JONAH WAS TENDING the one white rose that had sprung up behind his cabin when he heard Eli's anxious voice. "Jonah, where are you, Jonah?"

"Back here, behind the cabin."

Eli came to stand next to Jonah. "Jonah," he began.

"Eli, can't we just watch this flower?"

"Sure, Jonah, but not today, I have no patience. My kids are making me crazy. They don't listen. I ask them to stack the wood, but they don't. I ask them to bring water up from the well, but they don't. They don't do their chores and they don't help out at the store. I get so angry and rightfully so — I am their father, their parent. I need to educate them."

"So why are you here?" Jonah said, as he gently slid his fingers along the rose petals.

"Because I feel so terrible after I yell and shout at my children."

"Eli, getting angry at children is like pouring pebbles on a rose blossom and expecting the rose to bloom."

Eli looked at the white rose and thought about that image.

"Eli, you are a good parent and it is good for a parent to expect and demand of their children. Just do it without the pebbles."

———————— *Message* ————————

Getting angry is like pouring pebbles on
flowers and expecting them to bloom.

Exercise

I want to share something personal. My twenty-five years of marriage and years of parenting our five children have been an incredible opportunity for me to work on my anger issues. What I have come to realize is that most of the time, getting angry was about covering up what I was truly feeling. I cannot say that this is categorically true for all types of parental anger, but I believe it to be true for most parental anger.

Here are a few examples:

I express anger but really I am hungry as I have been so busy feeding everyone else.

I express anger but really I am tired as I have been so busy doing laundry and things for my children.

I express anger but really I am upset at what my friend just told me on the phone.

I express anger but really I am disappointed that my child isn't listening to me.

I express anger but really I am stressed about work or my weight.

Notice how anger is actually a cover for feeling different varieties of weakness: hunger, tiredness, self-image, or esteem issues. Many parents think expressing their weaknesses makes them less of a parent. I think it makes them more humane and a better parent. Anger management is a huge parental challenge. For although anger is a proper tool to use when your child is about to do something dangerous, anger does not cause our children to grow. It suffocates them like pebbles do to a rose blossom.

If you are interested in not getting as angry as you do today, you can do so by learning to tell your children what you are feeling.

For example:

> I am very hungry.
> I am so tired.
> I am so upset.
> I am so disappointed.
> I am incredibly stressed.
> I am feeling very weak.

_____ *Affirmation* _____

I am strong enough to share that I am feeling weak.

Battling Wolves

ELI CONTINUED, "JONAH, I am scared. I do get angry. Sometimes I even feel my face getting red hot. You are right - my anger doesn't make my children want to spend more time or even talk with me. I am scared because I get angry, and lots of times rightfully so, but I keep thinking about those pebbles and how they will choke the flowers. It is like I have a battle inside of me. Get angry, or be firm and understanding? I keep battling with myself. I feel angry. Should I tell them? How I should tell them? And then BOOM! I am yelling. Jonah, help me!"

"Eli, we are so much alike. We both have two wolves living inside us. A good wolf and a bad wolf. The wolf of firm understanding, and the angry wolf. These wolves battle inside us our entire lives. The question of which wolf will be victorious depends on which wolf we feed."

—————— Message ——————

Doing good brings more good into your life.

174

Exercise

We are like magnets. If we do good, good comes to us. If we are nice to people, people will be nice to us. It is true that it may take some people more time to respond to our positive attitude, yet in the end most people will come around.

Doing good attracts good people into our lives. When we do good, life will also send us opportunities to do good. When we do good, we also create the awareness in our minds that directs us to do even better things.

For example: The heat goes out at my neighbors' house, so I host them for dinner and the night. My neighbors share with their neighbors how nice I was, and when the heat isn't working at the school, the teacher asks if you can host the PTA meeting. Being nice has presented you with more opportunities to be nice and has also expanded your capacity to be nice — going from one neighbor to the whole PTA.

Feeding the good wolf, i.e., being nice, is also helpful during a heated argument. If I express disagreement with a calmer voice, the other side will respond in kind.

Another example of this is when I am calmer at home, my home will be calmer.

- Experiment with lowering your voice during an argument.
- After work, before you enter your home, stand at your door and take a few calming breaths so your calmness will generate more calmness.
- Draw a "Quality Graph" depicting how a quality has de-

veloped and grown during your life. The graph should depict highs and lows of how this quality expressed itself in your life. Examples of qualities: Giving of my time, controlling my anger, being able to listen to other people, being sensitive to other people's needs.

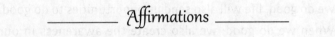

_____ *Affirmations* _____

I attract goodness into my life.

I attract calmness into my life.

The Traveler

A TRAVELER HAPPENED TO pass by Jonah's cabin and Jonah invited him for supper. The man sat in Jonah's one-room cabin and wondered why Jonah had so few belongings in his home.

"Jonah," he asked, "Why are your only possessions a table, a few books, a bed, two chairs, some dishes, and an icebox?"

Jonah replied, "I learned this from a very important person. You see, a disciple traveled for many months to visit an important Elder.

"The visitor asked the Elder, 'Why do you sit on a little wooden bench and have so few possessions?'

"The Elder asked the disciple, 'Tell me, where is your furniture?'

"The disciple said 'All I have with me now is this one suitcase because I am traveling.'

"The Elder smiled and explained, 'In this world, so am I just traveling.'"

——————— Message ———————

*We become too attached to our
physical possessions.*

Exercise

How many feet do you have?

Now count how many shoes you have.

We live in a culture of excess and, at times, lose the balance between surrounding ourselves with the physical possessions that we need and those which are in excess.

Look through your closets and donate one pair of excess shoes or one piece of clothing. If you are ready, go through more of your belongings and donate all the excess.

Affirmation

I am simplifying my attachment
to physical possessions.

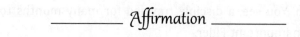

Brain Washing

DAVID WAS CURIOUS. "Jonah," he asked, "did you ever have any formal education?"

"You mean like going to a seminary?" asked Jonah.

"Yes," David replied.

"Well, David, as a child, my father instructed me. Yet I left home at age fourteen because there were too many tensions between us. It was four years before I returned home and was ready to go to seminary."

"But," David exclaimed. "I heard that seminary studies are so intense that one can be brainwashed by them!"

Jonah said, "Well, by that time I was hoping someone would wash my brain!"

———————— Message ————————

Sometimes we need to cleanse our thoughts.

Exercise

Sometimes we feel our thoughts need to be cleansed.

Possible sources of unclean thoughts may be condescending or degrading thoughts about others or ourselves, or ingesting information or visuals which we deem immoral, through the media, TV, or internet.

How can we cleanse our minds?

THE FIRST WAY:

Stop filling our minds with garbage.

We can achieve this by:

Going on a three-day media diet.

Refraining from gossip for one day.

Refraining from crude words for one day.

Notice when negative thoughts about yourself or others go through your mind. Counter them with a positive thought about yourself or another person.

THE SECOND WAY:

We can fill our brains with clean thoughts.

We can achieve this by:

Having a meaningful conversation.

Reading a magazine or book which contains wisdom.

Listening to uplifting music.

Listening to an audio self-help program.

Reading spiritual or religious literature.

—————— *Affirmations* ——————

I can cleanse my brain.

I can control my thoughts.

I am a qualified doorman. I decide what to keep
inside my brain and what to keep out.

The River Crossing

ONE DAY, THE Village Elder and Jonah went for a walk down to the river. Standing at the water's edge was a beautiful young woman wearing a fancy dress. She turned to them asking, "Could one of you please help me across the river?"

Jonah said, "Yes." The Elder was a little surprised because it was not modest for a man to carry a woman in his arms.

Jonah carried the woman across. On the other side of the river, Jonah gently put her down, and said goodbye to her.

Jonah and the Elder continued their walk. Two hours later, the Elder said to Jonah, "You know, I cannot get it out of my head. It really was not so modest to carry her."

To this Jonah replied, "I let her go two hours ago, but you are still carrying her."

_____ Message _____

*When a troubling experience is
over, we need to let it go.*
_____

Exercise

Even though troubling experiences may have happened two hours ago, two years ago, or twenty years ago, we tend to hold on to them and continue to carry them. These troubling experiences tend to weigh us down, tie us to our past, and not allow us to engage our future.

Pathways to stop carrying old, troubling experiences:

- Sometimes, it is only the passing of time that helps us let go.
- Therapeutic intervention can help us let go of a troubling past experience.
- Self-introspection of how we benefited from this troubling experience can allow us to stop obsessing about what happened to us and let go.
- Here is a calming visualization that you might find helpful: Close your eyes and envision a clear glass. See yourself dipping the glass into a river of drinkable water. The glass is now full of drinkable water, but there is also sediment in the glass. If you mix the water up, you will not be able to drink the water. Yet if you allow the water to settle, the sediment will sink to the bottom and you will be able to drink the water.

So it is with our minds. If we continue to think about all our troubles, present and past, we become a mixture of water and sediment. When we rest our minds, the confusion sinks and our minds become clear.

——— *Affirmations* ———

I free my mind of troubling thoughts.

I allow my mind to rest.

Climbing Higher

SOMETIMES JOSEPH WOULD help Jonah with his wood chopping. Jonah always welcomed Joseph's help. But as Jonah was a cautious man, he stood a little farther away when Joseph was chopping the wood, just in case Joseph's drinking had made his hand unsteady. After the work, Joseph always promised that he would not use the money to buy a drink, and Jonah would give Joseph a few coins for his effort.

A few months later, after so many, many, many hugs and "honest" coins earned from chopping wood, Joseph was able to find himself a full-time job. Joseph's new work was loading and unloading the stagecoach. Late at night, Joseph would still join Jonah around his fire. Looking down at his coffee cup, Joseph thought about all the time he had lost in his drinking glass.

He said, "Jonah, I am so jealous of all the regular people who have climbed so high in their lives and I am just beginning."

Jonah warmed his hands in front of the fire and said, "You know, Joseph, when you see two people on a mountain and one person is standing higher than the other one, to be able to answer the question: 'Who climbed further?', you would first have to know from where each person started!"

There is more discouragement than
encouragement to be gained by
comparing ourselves to others.

Exercise

One of the ways we sabotage ourselves is by comparing our actions to others. This is self-sabotage because there is always someone who is more something than we are: more successful, wealthier, healthier, thinner, prettier, calmer, more creative, has more self-control, has a more sensitive wife/husband, has better-behaved children.

Thinking about how other people are more successful and then thinking about ourselves, directs our attention away from the real issue which is where am I and where do I want to be.

There is an adage which says, it is very difficult for someone to be 100% of who they can be, but it is possible for me to be 100% of who I am, today.

The exercise is to encourage ourselves by comparing our present self with our past self — comparing who I am today with who I was twelve months ago.

Make yourself a chart:

	My previous self – last year	*My current self*
Financially		
Spiritually		
Relationships		
Emotional development		
Interests		

——————— *Affirmation* ———————

I celebrate how high I have climbed.

When I choose to focus on my mistakes, I do so tenderly.

Growing Old

HINDI, ONE OF the Village Elders, went to visit Jonah. She watched Jonah methodically place a chunk of wood on his chopping block, split it into two, place the two pieces on the woodpile and then repeat the same thing all over again with another chunk of wood. Hindi noticed that Jonah's swing was not as swift as it had been ten years earlier when he first came to the village. Teasingly, she said, "Jonah, are you growing old?"

Jonah looked at Hindi, smiled and replied, "Hindi, either you are growing or you are old, but you cannot be both."

Message

You get old when you stop developing.

Exercise

Being alive has little to do with breathing. Many people breathe, yet do not feel alive.

The same is true regarding aging. Aging has little to do with chronology. There are many people who have lived relatively few years chronologically, yet feel old. And there are those who have lived many years, but feel energetic and youthful.

To feel young and alive, one needs to answer these questions:

Choose one area in your life:

How would you like to develop it?
What will help you develop it? Who will help you develop it?
How will you increase or preserve your physical energy?
What will inspire you to develop emotionally?

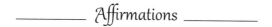 *Affirmations*

I look forward to developing all the
different spheres of my life.

As I age, I grow in wisdom and experience.
I celebrate this process.

The Next Step

DAVID NOTICED JONAH'S broad, strong shoulders from years of chopping wood. David then wondered what chopping wood with Jonah, for ten years, had done to his own shoulders.

After chopping wood together for an hour, David lowered his axe and finally said what had been on his mind, "Jonah, we have been together for a very long time. I have listened to the advice you have given to many, many people, and I learned from the manner in which you have shared your wisdom. I believe that your wisdom is true. I believe that one could build a life based on your wisdom, but I do not want to listen anymore."

"David, don't be afraid of growing slowly. Be afraid only of standing still."

"I understand that, but now I want it to be my time."

Jonah just continued chopping and said, "Make it your time, David."

"But, Jonah, tell me, what is the next step?" David implored.

Jonah lowered his axe, rubbed wood shards off his hands and said, "As you know, David, there is a custom that when all else fails, we ask the Elder to pray on our behalf. You may not know this, but Anna Goodman was married a long time before she had a baby. Anna would faithfully go to the Village Elder year after year, asking for God's help. Every year, the Elder would tell Anna the same thing, 'At the end of the year, you will have a baby.' I think it took ten years until she finally had her first child. Meanwhile, Rebecca Hertzberg started going to the Elder with the same request and received the same answer, but she had a baby one year later. Although Anna was happy for Rebecca, she was upset with the Elder. Anna questioned the Elder, 'Why did I have to wait such a long time, while Rebecca's plea was answered immediately?' The Elder replied, 'The difference is, when I told Rebecca that within the year her prayer would be answered, she went out and bought a baby carriage.'"

——— Message ———
Action creates realities.

Exercise

Make a list of how you want your life to be different regarding finances, relationships, physical fitness, education. Choose one area. Decide on one specific small step you need to take to improve your situation. Take that small step. Once completed, take another small step.

If there is a change you want to happen, change your

behavior so you begin to act like the change you want. This is what is known as a self-fulfilling prophecy.

_____ Affirmations _____

I am going forward.

Doing something is more than not doing anything.

———————— ⚜ ————————

Nearsighted Lanterns

"JONAH, IT IS time for me to go off on my own path. I feel that I am ready to leave, yet my path is unclear. When I leave our village, I will always know where I came from, but I don't know exactly where I am headed."

"David, do you remember when we used to go for walks at night in the forest, and the lanterns we held?"

"Of course."

"When we held the lanterns, they just lit up the next ten or fifteen paces and yet we were able to walk the whole way back to your home at the Elder's cabin.

"You see, our responsibility is to walk and hold the lantern. The lantern will give us the light we need for the next few steps. Once we have fulfilled our responsibility and walked the distance we can walk, then the lantern will once again respond with the gift of light for the next few steps."

——————— Message ———————

Focus on your next step and don't let completing the ultimate goal paralyze your walking.

Exercise

We all have a voice inside which trips us up. It is called the "Perfectionist Voice." The voice that says "What I do will never be good enough" or "I will never finish what I began."

It is the voice that says, "I don't have my life all figured out, so why try?"

This voice trips us up because:

- We cannot be perfect
- We don't have a perfect dream
- We don't have the perfect business/relationship idea, then why try at all.

In this story, we are introduced to the "Lantern Voice" that says do what you can and trust. When you are finished doing what you can do, you will see what you couldn't see before. When you work on your life, business, relationship, then life responds by showing you the next step. We would like life to show us all the next steps. We would like clarity for the next six to twelve months, yet it doesn't always work that way. Pick up the lantern. Enjoy its light for the next step, and by the time you have finished the next step, the lantern will show you the next step and the next and the next.

For example:

Problem	Lantern Steps
Teenage daughter is dealing with major issues	I can buy her a candy, I can have supper with her, I can take her shopping, I can give her a ride to the mall/school
Child is having school difficulties	I can make him hot chocolate, I can talk to his teacher, I can talk to other parents
Relationship is on the rocks	I can share a kind word, I can make a small gesture, and I can make a phone call or send an email.

Affirmations

I take pride in my small accomplishments.

I have the strength to take one step.

I trust that if I do, I will go forward.

What Should I Study?

THE DAY FINALLY came when David arrived with his knapsack. "Jonah, I am leaving. I am going off to the big city. I heard that in the city, they have a seminary and a university. I am going to work, find myself a trade, and study the world and the depths of life. I am so excited!"

Jonah's smile filled his face. "David, I am so happy for you."

"But, Jonah, one last question – what should I study? What courses should I take? There are so many choices. What should I study?"

Years later, when David was asked the same question, he always answered with Jonah's words, the very words that were etched, forever, in his mind.

Jonah had answered David's question: "David, what you decide to study depends on who you want to become."

—— Message ——

We are what we study.

Exercise

Plan today for six months from now:
   Who do you want to be?

196

What skills do you want to acquire?

What are the issues you would like to resolve?

Decide today what you need to study in order to achieve your six-month goal.

Now, divide your six-month goal in half. How will things be different three months from today? What will cause them to be different?

Now, speculate on the end of the first month. What change do you foresee by the end of the first month?

Now, plan the first week. What are you going to do during the first week to get the ball rolling?

Now, focus on today. What is the next small step you are going to take today?

Do not allow your six-month goal to paralyze you.

Keep focusing on the small steps and good luck.

We both know you can take a small step.

Just keep on taking them.

Affirmations

Through study, I have the power to
bring my future into the present.

I am attracting my future.

The Unlovable

AFTER DAVID LEFT, Jonah felt that something had ended and it was also time for him to move on.

He told the Elder of his plan to quietly slip away and asked the Elder to keep his intention in confidence. Yet the Elder couldn't let Jonah go without some expression of how much comfort his wisdom had brought to the village. On the planned day, Jonah awoke to the voice of many whisperings. Looking out his window, he saw the whole village had turned out to say goodbye.

Jonah had gone to sleep packed and ready to leave, so he quickly gathered himself, said thank you to his cabin for its shelter, and closed its door.

He approached his friends, reaching out to take their hands and hugs. Jonah was amazed how much love meeting eyes can share, and how much one can cry without shedding a tear.

Jonah didn't know what to say so he said nothing as he slowly walked towards the forest.

Finally, Sarah said "Bye" and Jonah turned, smiled and waved.

They watched him walk into the forest and were quiet for quite some time.

Finally Jonah disappeared among the trees and Eli broke

the silence. "I am going to miss having coffee with him."

Saul said, "I learned so much from him."

Others shared similar sentiments and bit by bit everyone went back to start their day until only one person was left. It was Joseph, and if one had gotten close enough, they would have heard his silent plea, "Who will love me now?"

_____ *Message* _____

Our love means so much to those who receive it.

_____

Exercise

If a president of a country would walk into a room, people would take notice. They would want to speak to or shake the president's hand. Yet what about the cleaner who cleaned the room? Who notices him? Who wants to speak to or shake his hand? When we enter a room and ignore the people that are there, we are essentially saying, "For me you do not exist." Ignoring someone is tantamount to denying their existence, while noticing people is an initial expression of love.

We may not want to love a drunk like Joseph, yet we can find room in our hearts to not ignore him.

This week, take time to notice the unnoticed people who surround you such as: the street cleaner, the garbage collector, or the janitor.

Maybe you can offer them a cup of coffee or a friendly "good morning."

Affirmations

I have so much love in my heart.

I share my love freely.

A New Woodchopper?

JOSEPH WENT LOOKING for Jonah and found him deep inside the forest.

"Jonah, wait. Wait for me."

Jonah stopped, realizing Joseph needed one more lesson.

"Jonah, I want to go with you."

"Why, Joseph?"

"Why? You know why. I need you. I need your hugs and your encouragement."

"Joseph, what do you need?"

"I told you, I need you, Jonah."

"Joseph, what do you really need from me?"

"Love. I need someone to love me and you loved me. Even when I smelled, even when I fell down – you loved me. "

"Joseph, love is a powerful medicine, and so many people need the healing that love brings. Joseph, it is time for me to move on and for you to go back. I am asking you to become the champion of that which you need. I am asking you to find kind words to share with people. To be the one who compliments and encourages."

"But I am not Jonah the woodchopper."

"This is true, but you are Joseph, and the village needs someone to chop wood."

---------- *Message* ----------

Become the champion of that which you need.

Exercise

Your life experience has made you realize how much you miss that which you didn't receive. For example, as a child you didn't receive enough love, appreciation, recognition, respect, money, etc.

Your life experience has made you realize how much you miss these things and how much you need them in your life. Your life experience has also made you sensitive enough to recognize these needs in others.

The hard fact to face is that your past isn't going to change. If you didn't receive something as a child, that is not going to change because you can't erase the past. You can, however, change the way you view your past. Through therapy you can break negative patterns so your past will not have a negative impact on your present or future, thereby not allowing your past to control your present or future.

What you can't do is erase the past. What you can do is change your future. At times, we need to deal with our past which is like cleaning up the dark stains, and at times, we need to work on our future which is like turning on a light so the dark stains aren't so significant anymore.

At the end of *Jonah*, we are focused on the future. We

are focused on what we can do to move our lives forward. We have spent time cleaning up the dark stains and now we want to turn on the light. At times, we can make our futures so bright that it dims a difficult past. Focus on what you can do. Be the change you want in this world. Create that which was missing from your life. Create it for yourself and for others, and then you will become the champion of that which you need.

For example:

I didn't receive	Become the champion of that which you need
Parents didn't develop your interests	Enroll yourself in self improvement classes, learn a musical instrument, or take up ceramics
Parents didn't spend enough time with me	Spending time with children
Parent was emotionally disengaged	Learn how to share your emotions
Difficult teenage years	Work with troubled teenagers
I didn't have a big brother	Become a big brother to others
I had teachers who weren't encouraging	Be encouraging
	Initiate compliments

_____Affirmations_____

I am focused on what I need.

I am taking smalls steps to obtain
what I need.

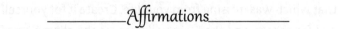

Thank You for the Stories

THANK YOU TO my magnificent wife, Annette, my partner in life. Together you and I have woven the most beautiful and poignant story of our shared lives. Thank you to my sweet, beloved children: Avi, Shayna, Yonatan, Shira, and Talya. My dear children, you ARE my story. We have shared around-the-dinner-table stories and bedtime stories. The magic I saw in your eyes reflected the awe I felt in my heart.

Thank you to my cherished father, Aba. You are the one who continually told me stories – many, many stories. Your stories were always deep, life narratives. Each story contained a parable and a message from which to learn a valuable lesson. Aba, these are the stories that made the spirit and the essence of my childhood so meaningful and significant. Your stories helped mold me into becoming the person I am today.

Thank you, Aba, for playing old radio programs during our daily hour ride to school. It was these radio programs, like *The Shadow*, *The Lone Ranger*, *The Inner Sanctum*, and *Abbot and Costello* that filled my mind with the imagery and dialogue that contributed to my talent for storytelling.

Thank you to my Ima, my loving mother, for loving me. Jonah's acceptance of those in need and his ability to take them into his heart is a tribute to how you treated all who knew you. It was your love of Broadway musicals that instilled in me a sense of theatrical drama found in the stories' cadence.

Thank you God, our Creator, for giving us Your Bible,

which begins with Your stories. The stories in the Bible make use of simple words, yet these simple words create the most vital stories, impregnated with the deepest spiritual and ethical lessons and values to guide humanity.

Thank you to Rabbi Shlomo Carlebach for his stories. Shlomo was the first rabbi I met who loved me and every-one else he met. My story, "The Hug," is based on Rabbi Shlomo's life.

Thank you to Rabbi Shlomo Riskin, who is an exemplary model in the art of dramatic storytelling and taught all of us rabbinical students how to be effective educators by sharing stories. The story "Where is the Love" is based on a true episode from Rabbi Riskin's rabbinical career.

Thank you to Rabbi Shlomo Kimche, who by sharing his stories, brought sanctity and purity to our shared university lunches.

Thank you to the Chassidic tradition of storytelling with its beautiful tales that warmed the hearts of so many souls on those oh-so-cold, wintry, European nights. I have reworked some of these lovely, traditional narratives and integrated them into the life-story of *Jonah the Woodchopper*. My stories "Burning Notebooks," "How Big Are Your Hands?" and "The Traveler" are examples of Chassidic folklore and storytelling.

I am thankful to the Eastern traditions that have shared so much of their wisdom with the West. Students of these traditions will recognize in some of my stories the teachings and insights of the Eastern way of life.

The story "Lovely Lettuce" is a true occurrence. Bryna Franklin sensed my annoyance as we were washing lettuce during a retreat. She then taught me the invaluable lesson of the story.

Thank you to Rabbi Avraham Sutton for sharing his special shining example and for his sweetness, his kindness, and his compassion. His encouragement has been a source of inspiration. I truly appreciate and thank him for ending our conversations with the words, "I love you."

Thank you to Rabbi Aryeh Ben-David. Your mentoring helped me shape *Jonah* into a guide through the forest of life.

Huge thanks to Yaakov Brody who went with me to the forest with an axe to act out Jonah. You helped me see how Jonah's fragilities would one day become his greatest source of power.

Thank you to Shmuel Bowman, Rabbi Avi Baumel, Tovah Leah Nachmani, Shana Mauer, Seth Merewitz, and Yonah Triestman. Your suggestions brought clarity and gave power to this creation.

Thank you to Vivian Friedman-Hachamoff for editing Jonah. You have brought clarity and smoothness to the stories.

Thank you to Barbara Clyman whose gift for preciseness has made Jonah crisp. Your remarks came with a passion and desire for Jonah to open and fix our hearts.

Thank you to the entire Penlight Publications team for your meticulous care with *Jonah*. Your efforts added clarity and calmness.

Thank you to all my kind friends who were so generous in sharing their stories: Rabbi David Aaron, Rabbi David Ebner, Rabbi Gedalyah Gurfien, Rabbi Menachem Schrader, and Rabbi Dovid Zeller.

A final thanks to my brother-in-law Howard Bressler, who taught me the lesson of living life generously, and without whose support this work would have never seen publication.

About the Author

JOSHUA RUBIN is a relationship guide, and personally coaches singles from dating to marriage. He has a graduate degree in Educational Counseling from Northeastern University in Boston, MA, was a student of Reb Shlomo Carlebach, and received rabbinic ordination from Rabbi Shlomo Riskin. Joshua is the author of *Spiritual Awakenings* in which he explores spirituality and the holidays, and *A Dad's Guide to Inspirational Parenting* in which he describes how fathers can become emotionally engaged parents. He is also a recording artist, having produced a CD "Sharing God's Softness" featuring himself on guitar and vocals.

Joshua is married to Annette, and they live in Israel with their five children. Joshua can be contacted through the website YehoshuaRubin.com.